# PERFECT PARTIES

# PERFECT PARTIES

## Second Edition

### Recipes and Tips from a New York Party Planner

*LINNEA JOHANSSON*

*Foreword by Marcus Samuelsson*

*Edited by Robert Andersson & Jared Levan*

*Photographs by Paul Brissman, Adrian Mueller & Stephen Murello*

*Jacket photography by Adrian Mueller, Morgan Norman & Evan Sung*

Skyhorse Publishing

Skyhorse Publishing books may be purchased in bulk at special discounts for sales promotion, corporate gifts, fund-raising, or educational purposes. Special editions can also be created to specifications. For details, contact the Special Sales Department, Skyhorse Publishing, 307 West 36th Street, 11th Floor, New York, NY 10018 or info@skyhorsepublishing.com.

Skyhorse® and Skyhorse Publishing® are registered trademarks of Skyhorse Publishing, Inc.®, a Delaware corporation.

Visit our website at www.skyhorsepublishing.com.

10 9 8 7 6 5 4 3 2 1

Library of Congress Cataloging-in-Publication Data is available on file.

ISBN: 978-1-61608-867-5

Printed in China

# PERFECT PARTIES

# Contents:

# *FOREWORD*

*INVITING PEOPLE INTO* your home for a party is an intimate gesture. Suddenly you're exposed: everything from your cooking to your wallpaper is out in the open, and you immediately begin to worry if people are going to have fun, whether they'll like the soup, or whether they'll ask for vodka when you only have wine. Suddenly the decision to throw a party has become a stressor when it should be a joy.

But the people you've invited haven't come to critique you; they've come to learn more about you. So throwing a great party is really just a matter of demonstrating a little about who you are through the food, drinks, decoration, and music you select.

For me, in the restaurant world, every event is about proper planning. But for a party in your home, the key is to both plan well and to allow for a little improvisation. That's when the magic happens. People today don't expect to sit down and be served. People want to participate. When my grandmother threw a party, she worked in the kitchen all evening and sat down with her guests only over coffee. People get very uncomfortable that way today. A party where the host or hostess mingles and introduces people and is full of energy is more interesting and more fun for everyone.

We are as different as the parties we throw, and what I love about *Perfect Parties* is that it gives you such a variety, and offers them in a dazzling display of visual creativity. Linnea covers everything from recipes to themes to flowers to place settings. She even touches on clothing to wear at your parties. Throwing a party is a way to express yourself; Linnea's gift to her readers is that she can inspire you with possibilities.

Everything in this book is based on classic party ideas. But Linnea adds her own creative twists which will wow your guests without overwhelming them. She makes hamburgers out of foie gras. They come with French fries, too, served with wasabi mustard and curry ketchup. She bakes cupcakes for dessert but adds chocolate truffles. She recommends mixed fruit for brunch, but grilled and on a skewer. With Linnea, tired ideas become new again, so you can still have your traditional brunch or barbeque, infused with imagination and flair.

Linnea and I have been working (and partying) in New York for many years. It is a wonderful place because there are so many different people from so many different cultures. You'll never be short on good party ideas here. But the biggest challenge for a New Yorker planning a party at home is that space is limited, especially kitchen space. Don't let that prevent you from throwing a great party. Linnea has some great ideas on how to work with what you have.

*Perfect Parties* is a wonderful book that can add some celebrity glamour to your everyday life. Linnea has been inspired by her many famous clients over the years. Now, it's her turn to inspire you. Read this book, and get ready to throw a perfect party.

> – Marcus Samuelsson
> Chef & Owner
> Red Rooster Harlem

# PLANNING

*T*urning Central Park Zoo into a lavish party venue is no easy task. For me, it was one of the most challenging events I have ever pulled together as a New York party planner. With more than four thousand invitations sent out, this party had to be impressive—and impressive it was.

The penguin house was turned into a caviar bar, the polar bear den into a sushi station, and the sea lion cave into a concert hall, complete with an opera singer. But that's not all. More than a thousand colorful silk pillows were designed and made specifically for the occasion to add comfort and warmth to the otherwise bare park benches while pink Chinese lanterns dangled from trees throughout the zoo, spreading a romantic glow for all to see. It was as surreal as a scene from a Tim Burton movie—it took your breath away.

Parties of this magnitude can give even the most experienced party planner nightmares. No matter how hard one may try to throw the "perfect" party, there is always something that may go awry. The truth is, there really is no such thing as the perfect party—and that's OK. Even great parties have their snags, and despite a few "inconveniences," my party at the zoo was a success, so much so that it ended up being nominated as one of the best that year.

# CREATIVE PLANNING

WHETHER *your guest list includes three or three thousand, the process is always the same when planning a party, and it starts with creative planning. Where will the party take place? What is your décor going to look like? What type of drinks will be served? The answer to these questions, and many others, will help you decide the concept and theme for any type of party and are the focus of creative planning. As a rule of thumb, for normal-sized events with 3–25 invited guests, you'll want to start this process at least four weeks in advance. If the party will be a larger event, you'll need to start your creative planning earlier.*

*Just remember, the goal of any planner should always be to plan a party that can be enjoyed by you and your guests where, for a few hours, you can hang out and experience something out of the ordinary together. Sound difficult? It's not. Ask yourself these eight simple questions the next time you want to throw a party and you'll be amazed at how simple it really is!*

*First, start with the most important question:*

## 1. WHY THROW A PARTY?

Maybe you got a new job and want to get to know your co-workers better. Perhaps you recently started your own business and could use a write up in the local paper. Whatever the occasion, the reason why you are throwing a party is one of the most important questions there is to ask because it decides how your party will evolve. And because every event is different, it's no surprise that each aspect of planning can differ as well. For example, an event thrown with a specific goal in mind, like getting publicity or raising money for a good cause, differs from parties thrown just for fun. In this case, the guest lists for both events will be very different. This book focuses primarily on throwing parties for friends and family.

### Don't be bashful.

Bored with nothing to do? Don't just sit around and wait for a birthday or wedding announcement. There are plenty of other reasons you can plan a celebration. Look around and you will find tons of reasons to throw a party to make your everyday life a little bit more fun, a little bit more often.

– You want to celebrate the end of winter and beginning of spring. Buy flowerpots, dirt, and seeds and throw a gardening party to usher in a new season of new growth! (Spring officially starts close to March 21 each year.)
– You're sick of the cold and dark winter, but it's February. Cheer up! February is also the month when Carnival kicks off in Rio. Play samba music, pass around spicy hors d'oeuvres, and kick up the heat to fight off the chill of the weather outside.
– You've subscribed to a food magazine for over a year now. Isn't it time to try out your impressive new culinary skills on your closest friends? Invite them to a three-course dinner and wow them with your mastery in the kitchen.
– It's fall, and your front yard is a mess! Invite your friends over for some apple picking and leaf raking, then return the favor with a delicious fall-themed brunch.

## Party for PR

In cities like New York City and Los Angeles, companies often throw extraordinary parties to get valuable media exposure and million-dollar budgets aren't unheard of—good PR is priceless! Do you run your own company, or are you devoted to a nonprofit organization that could really use some press coverage? Invite local media reps from the paper, TV, or high-traffic blogs to a press breakfast, tea party, or whatever kind of function you find suitable. You'll have a great opportunity to talk about your business or organization and the press, in return, will be able to ask questions and spread the word. Always have a theme for an event like this and announce it on the invitation. For example, fall's new flower trends will be shown and explained in your flower shop, or a club's new soccer coach will be introduced. Keep the gathering short and preferably during the week. This way, writers and journalists get as much time as possible to work on a piece before deadline. The event should be held in a public space, not in your own home. Most importantly, you'll want to let friends and family know that this is a business event—professionals only on the guest list!

## 2. WHAT TYPE OF PARTY?

When it comes to choosing the type of party you want to throw, the options are endless. With any type, however, you'll want to avoid making your party more ambitious than your schedule allows. It should be fun to plan, not another stressful task on your already packed "to-do" list. Remember, there are always great short cuts you can use. Having difficulties fitting in that three-course dinner between work, yoga, and your weekly pottery class? There's no need to abandon your idea altogether. Instead of stressing over a lavish meal, try buying some marshmallows, graham crackers, and chocolate bars and invite your guests to a s'mores BBQ. It may not be dinner, but it's bound to be a whole lot of fun!

## 3. GUESTS?

Now that you've chosen a reason to plan a party and what type of party you want to throw, whom will you invite? The guest list of any party will vary based on your answers to the previous questions, so try to go in order! Deciding how many guests you want to invite in the early stages of planning allows you to easily plan the party's budget, choose the venue, and decided the food and drink menus. Diversity is great, especially when it comes to party guests, so be sure to always invite a mix of old and new faces for a dynamic and fun event. The smaller the engagement, the more time and thought it takes to achieve the right mix of guests. For a press event, you might want to kindly turn away friends and family so you can focus on the task at hand. Charity functions, on the other hand, are the perfect occasion to invite your friends—especially if they have a little extra cash.

## 4. TIMING?

Be open-minded while deciding when the party will take place—there's no rule saying it has to be at night. It's just as nice to meet and greet in the middle of the day as it is after dark. Party timing is very important as it affects the type of food you are expected to serve. If you don't have the time or budget to cook lots of food, it's perfect to throw a late-night cocktail party. Guests will have eaten before they arrive, and you can simply serve canapés that look luxurious but are simple to make and friendly to your wallet. To avoid awkward misunderstandings or starving guests, give a hint on the invitation as to what will be served. For example, Canapé and Cocktails, Dessert Buffet, Wine & Finger Foods . . . and so on.

## 5. BUDGET?

It's easy to get carried away when it comes to party expenses, but you won't enjoy yourself much if you end up eating mac and cheese for weeks in advance, just to compensate for overspending on Champagne and caviar. Therefore, make a budget before you proceed with your party plans by writing down how much you want to spend, then add 10% as an emergency buffer for unexpected costs. Figuring out your budget early will leave plenty of time to call different stores to compare prices, and can truly make a difference when it comes to your total cost. Another cost-saving technique any party planner learns to use is the "DIY" approach. For example, if you're good at creating flower arrangements, why not make your own? If so, use most of the décor budget on fresh flowers and greenery. Are you an amazing cook? Spend most of your money on food, and so on. If you are a notorious overspender, withdraw your budgeted amount and keep the money in an envelope, paying all your expenses in cash. When the envelope is empty you're done shopping, even if things are missing. That's the law! (Hint: always start with the most important things first.)

## 6. VENUE?

An important aspect of any party that can affect how much time and effort you have to put into your party preparations is the venue you choose. When it comes to planning, there are three major types of location: your home, a restaurant/catering hall, and raw-venues, all of which have their pros and cons. Restaurants are practical venue options but they are easily over-priced and it can be difficult to maintain the atmosphere you're going for with restuarant patrons in the mix. Raw-venues are even more expensive since you have to arrange everything from furniture and decorations to lighting and food, which means you'll be putting a lot more time and planning into the event. The upside of any raw-venue, however, is that it allows you to create exactly the atmosphere you want. Outdoor spaces are another type of raw-venue that can prove to be amazing—if the weather is on your side. In the unfortunate event the weather is poor, however, you're in a bind. Most times, you will find the best venue for a party is in the comfort of your own home. There's no rental fee, you can fit more

guests than you think, the furniture and kitchen are in place, and you can easily create a new mood with the right lighting and decorations.

## 7. FOOD AND BEVERAGE?

Now that you've answered the previous questions, it's time to decide what type of food and beverages you'd like to serve at the upcoming party. Determining the menu for a party should be no more stressful than any other aspect of party planning, so keep your dishes simple, and make sure most items on the menu can be prepared in advance. This way you're not stuck in the kitchen all evening and you can mingle with your guests, as a host should!

## 8. YOUR TWIST?

What makes any run-of-the-mill party go from simple to extraordinary? A theme! Even with the same menu, guest list, and budget of another party, a theme will help you create a unique experience so memorable that your guests will talk about it for weeks. So what kinds of themes are there? They can be as simple as a color theme, or a more advanced theme where you transform your home into a tropical oasis—cabanas, piña coladas, and all. Planning with a theme in mind not only adds a twist that makes your party special, but it also helps provide inspiration. No matter what your theme, it should be reflected in everything you do, from the invitation design to the dessert choice.

### What to Eat When?

Among the many things there are for the perfect party host to know, one is that certain foods should only be served at certain hours—so memorize the information below. The chart's time intervals indicate between which hours the party should start:

9–11 AM: Breakfast

11 AM–1 PM: Lunch/ Brunch

2–4 PM: Tea party

5–9 PM: Cocktail party

6–9 PM: Dinner/Buffet

# PRACTICAL PLANNING

CONGRATULATIONS! ONCE YOU'VE *answered all eight questions in the creative planning phase, you now have a great party concept. Now it's time for the next step in the process: practical planning. During this phase, you'll take all your great ideas and make them a reality. Everything from making the invitations and sending them out on time, to calculating when the rice goes on the stove so it's ready at the same time as the chicken entree. The more exact you are with your practical planning, the smoother your party will run and the more time you'll have to enjoy yourself. As with creative planning, it's best to start with practical planning approximately four weeks before your event. Use this "slacker's guide," or cheat sheet, to avoid forgetting any important details or loose ends.* (See p. 19)

*First aid for an event planner is a toolbox overflowing with gear such as staple and glue guns, tape measures, adhesive tape, Band-Aids, and other indispensable equipment.*

# Slacker's Party Guide

*Use this slacker's guide to help plan a party in your own home. If it's a truly grand occasion, like a wedding or a family reunion, keep in mind that you'll need much more than four weeks to prep for the celebration. Every party is different, so use this guide only as a model, then mold it to fit your specific needs.*

## 4 weeks before

- Decide on a theme.- Pick your venue
- Measure the space where your event will be held.
- Draw a floor plan and make sure all your party décor fits.
- Design the invitations.
- Create a budget.

## 3 weeks before

- Send out the invitations.
- Decide on menu and beverages.
- Make a shopping list with approximated costs and compare it with your budget.

## 2 weeks before

- Plan the décor in detail and where you can find needed materials.
- Approximate your décor costs. Compare with budget.

## 1 week before

- Verify your RSVP list. Call or send emails to guests you haven't heard from.
- Buy beverages and decorations, except flowers and other perishables.
- Call your florist. Make sure what you need is in stock or can be ordered.
- Borrow or rent extra equipment like chairs, tables, and china if needed.

## 2 days before

- Make a "service schedule." Write down your exact plan for the event and be as precise as possible. For example, which food and drinks are you going to serve, and at what hour? The schedule will help you find things you might have forgotten about and make your party run smoothly.
- Purchase the food.
- Double-check your shopping lists and make sure that you have everything you need.
- Decide what to wear to avoid last minute fashion stress.

## The day before

- If you are having a seated dinner, make your seating arrangements. Don't make it sooner since last minute changes and cancellations are common.
- Pick up the flowers if you are creating your own flower arrangements.
- Prepare all décor, except flower arrangements.
- Set the tables and make sure everything fits.
- Set up the bar(s).
- Prepare as much of the food as possible.

## The day of the party!

- Create the flower arrangements in the morning.
- Buy ice.
- Get some good music going and cook the rest of your food.
- Chill the bottled beverages that are supposed to be served cold. It takes about 30 minutes for a 25 oz. bottle of wine to cool down in an ice bath.
- Get dressed and have all preparations done except last minute food one hour prior to your party. Make all final preparations, sip on a drink, and double-check everything—twice if it will make you feel better.
- Welcome your guests and let the party begin!

# Balance Your Budget

Divide your budget into separate expense groups, and write down different costs under its corresponding group. When done, add all your costs together and there it is: your budget.

Invitations: Cards, envelopes, pencils, and other supplies needed for your invitations. Don't forget to include postage.

Food: Everything edible that is served at the party.

Beverages: Everything drinkable, and everything you need when garnishing your cocktails (lime wedges, straws, etc.).

Décor: Candles, flowers, light bulbs, tablecloths, table seating cards, napkin rings, fabrics, napkins—in short, anything and everything used to decorate the event.

Entertainment: Music, the fee for your favorite local rock band, a belly dancer, a DJ, the DVD for movie night, games for board game night, rented speakers, and so on.

Other Expenses: Venue fees, rented china, glasses, tables and chairs, wait staff, photographer fees, cleaning products, extra toiletries, and other costs that pop up and don't fit under any of the other expense categories.

10% Buffer: The unexpected does happen, especially when planning a party. Be prepared by adding up all of your costs and adding 10 percent to your budget to use as a buffer for last minute expenses.

*Planning is key to a successful party. Get a big folder out, and start collecting all your information and facts for the event; the budget, telephone numbers, sketches of your decorations, ideas for the menus, and shopping lists.*

# GUESTS

*A**s a professional event planner, you meet a lot of celebrities and over the years I've learned that they all have very different preferences. Donald Trump doesn't drink alcohol, but loves Swedish meatballs. Nelson Mandela likes spicy food, while Salma Hayek detests curry. In hindsight, some encounters have been more pleasant than others. At one party I inadvertently bumped into Woody Allen so hard that he ended up crumpled on the floor, and at a fashion event I lost my assistant when Justin Timberlake hired him as his new background dancer on the spot—just more evidence that no matter how much you plan, anything—and I mean anything—can happen.*

*With any well-planned event, it's important to remember that different types of parties call for different types of guests. For instance, when organizing a gala or launch party, it's crucial to get interesting or well-known guests to attend since companies spend a lot of money on those types of events, sometimes even millions of dollars.*

*Because celebrities may get invited to several parties a day, you'll want to create an invitation that stands out from all the rest in order to get their attention. Gift bags never hurt either. Once I sent out one pearl earring as part of the invitation; the matching earring was given to the guests as they arrived at the party. I've also delivered flowers with invitations in the bouquet, praline boxes with party essentials written on the bonbons, and I've even sent people off to the tailor where they've had their measurements taken for a free custom-made shirt scheduled to arrive after the event. Perhaps the most expensive gift bag I've ever handed out, however, was a specially-designed Burberry bag that contained luxurious products worth tens of thousands of dollars.*

# MIX IT UP

YOU CAN COOK *a buffet with the most sensational of flavors and transform your living room into a lavish oasis, but no matter what, it is still the guests that set the tone of your party. Always follow the "golden rule" of party planning and invite a mix of old and new faces to make things more interesting for you and your guests. Let's be honest — everyone appreciates an invitation to a party! So although it may feel a bit uncomfortable inviting people you aren't best buds with at first, it's worth mustering up the courage for. When it comes time for the party, you'll quickly see how a dynamic group of guests will create new friendships, inspire interesting conversations, and offer great networking opportunities for your guests. There are, however, exceptions to the golden rule. If you're planning a more intimate event such as your friends' bridal shower, for instance, you'd only want to invite close friends and familiar faces.*

## Party Memories

Create a fun party memento by leaving a guest book on the table at your next event and ask your friends to write something down before they leave; you're bound to receive plenty of great feedback!. As an added bonus, keep a Polaroid camera next to the book so guests can take their pictures as well. Attach the pictures in the book or give them as gifts to your guests as souvenirs.

# Q&A About Guests

**What should I do if someone calls last minute and asks to bring extra guests?**

As the saying goes, "the more the merrier," and in most cases that absolutely holds true when having a party—but it's also OK to say no. A seated dinner with extra guests might, for example, require major rearrangements or a higher budget in order to buy more food. One option to avoid stressful, last-minute changes is to invite the extra guests to join you for dessert or after dinner cocktails. In the event you do allow for extra guests, be prepared! Always have extra bread, cheese, snacks, and dip for your buffet or cocktail party. As a rule of thumb, keep in mind that most people prefer to RSVP + 1.

**Do I really have to invite all my relatives to important occasions like birthdays or weddings?**

Not really, but always be cautious when it comes to family. You can easily hurt someone's feelings if you invite just a few of your relatives and leave others out.

**Can I pull back invitations that have already been sent out when I realize I've invited too many people?**

No, but you can save face gracefully if someone RSVPs last minute or after the set date. Tell them that you are sad to have to inform them that the response has been greater than you expected, and that the guest list has already been filled up. If everyone RSVPs on time you have to bite the bullet.

**What should I do if a guest doesn't follow the dress code written on the invitation?**

Don't judge a book by its cover (especially not this one). If you really want everyone to follow a specific dress code, such as for a theme party, stock up on extra masks, flowers, and other suitable props so you're well prepared when guests show up and haven't dressed the part.

**If I write an RSVP date on the invitation, can I expect everyone to reply, even the ones that can't attend?**

Of course! As a host, if you've taken the time to invite someone, that person can take the time to get back to you—even if he or she can't make it. If you haven't heard from people a week before your party, go ahead and call or email to ask if they received their invitation, and confirm if they plan to attend or not.

**My feet hurt and it's getting late. How do I get my guests to leave?**

Set up a small coffee bar for your late-nighters. The same way coffee after a meal signals that dinner is over, this gesture hints that the party will soon come to an end. If this doesn't work, try slowly turning down the music and even discreetly switching on a few lights in the room. Whatever you do, don't start cleaning until all your guests have left. Another foolproof way to avoid lingering guests is to state the hours of your party on the invitation. This is especially recommended for daytime or early evening affairs.

# THE INVITATION

ONCE YOU'VE SETTLED *on what old and new faces you want to see at your party, it's time to invite them. Put effort and thought into your invitation since it will be the guests' first impression of your affair. Let the invitation design reflect your party's theme and give a glimpse of the extraordinary party to come. Think of it as marketing.*

*An eye-catching invitation is the best way to ensure a great turnout at any celebration. Need help getting started? There are plenty of free online invitation services that offer an inexpensive and quick way to send out your invitations. It's also convenient for you and your guests to RSVP via email as you can easily tally up how many guests have agreed to attend and how many have declined. An extra treat is that the guests can keep in touch online, and you can send out reminders as the big day (or night) draws closer.*

*E-vites may be simple to create and manage, but nothing creates bigger buzz for an occasion than a traditional paper invitation. You'll want to decide how important the invitation is for the party you are having and how much time and money you are prepared to spend on it. If you're celebrating the season premiere of your favorite TV series, an email with a retouched picture of you, posing with your favorite star, should be enough. For a twentieth anniversary or other grand affair, a paper invitation is definitely more suitable. After all, it's a big occasion, and a paper invite gives a more serious impression to guests. A third alternative is to call and invite your guests over the phone when throwing a smaller gathering. It's less expensive than a paper invitation, it's much more personal that an e-mail, and you'll generally get a "yes" or a "no" while you're on the phone!*

## CLASSIC INVITATION

THERE ARE TWO *types of invitations—classic and creative. Go for a classic invitation when throwing a milestone event, like a baptism, wedding, or fiftieth anniversary. It may also be suitable for a glamorous themed party, like your own Oscar party or Nobel Prize banquet.*

*Because classic invitations suggest a grander event, the language on the card should be short and direct. Instead of writing out all of your punctuation, start new sentences on a new line. It's a good idea to state the event's attire, even if there isn't one, just to avoid confusion and stress over what to wear. You can order custom-made classic invitations online, or in your local paper shop. When buying in a shop, you can ask for help to ensure you get the quality and design you like. If you are on a budget you can easily make your own beautiful knock-off classic invitations at home. Choose a paper of thicker quality—this will give a luxurious feel to your invite. Before starting with your self-made card design, head down to the paper store to get ideas and inspiration by looking through their books and selection.*

### RULES FOR A CLASSIC INVITATION

#### Color
White or cream-colored paper and matching envelopes.

#### Size
The card should be 4x6 inches, or 5x7 inches.

#### Design
Keep it simple, preferably with a border around the text. Border and text should be the same color.

#### Motif
This is an optional small graphic symbol that matches the occasion.

#### Monogram
Optional—initials on the invitation.

#### Ink
Use one of the classic colors: black, dark blue, silver, or gold ink.

#### Text
Align the text to the left, or center it on the card.

#### Handwritten
Add a personal touch by writing the guest's name on the invitation or writing their address on the envelope by hand, preferably with a calligraphy pen.

### Card Facts 101

Are you on a spending spree and want to custom order beautiful invitations from your local paper store? Here are some useful expressions that might help you discuss the look of your card with the store expert.

Card stock—The thickness/weight of the paper, usually ranging from 65–100 pounds.

Engraved—A copper stamp is used to raise or lower the paper to create a symbol or text.

Thermography—A technique using chemicals in the ink to raise the text.

*CREATIVE INVITATION*

USUALLY THE RULE *of thumb is "The crazier, the better," but remember to stick to your theme. A creative invitation is perfect for a birthday or cocktail party and nowadays it's also common to send out creative invitations to parties that traditionally used to have only classic invitations—weddings and baby showers, for example. Decorate the invitations with dried flowers or satin ribbon for a more romantic look. Let your creativity and style decide what your invitation should look like, and don't hesitate to experi-ment with different card folds and color or paper choices. Instead of mailing invitation cards, you can also send out things that match your theme. Make the text fun and upbeat. It can even be a bit outrageous. Try to make lightweight invitations to keep your postage costs down.*

## Ideas for Creative Invitations

- Photos. Take snapshots of gadgets or yourself dressed up to match the party theme. Print them up in black and white, or in a brown tint, if you want to create an old-fashioned look. Glue or use photo corners to attach them to your cards and send them as your invitations.

- Things. Send a compass for a camping party, an oven mitt with the where and when to a barbeque gathering, flip-flops for a beach party, bingo trays welcoming a bingo evening, or a pacifier for the "It's A Boy" party.

- Telegram. A fun and unexpected way to invite your guests.

- Live Invitations. This is over the top, but if you've got the budget for it, don't hesitate to send out live invitations. Have a flower messenger deliver invitations to the midsummer night's party in his bouquets, have an opera singer belt out the info for your operetta evening on the guests' doorsteps, or hire a belly dancer to invite your friends to an exotic Turkish brunch while shaking her hips.

## INVITATION ETIQUETTE/KNOW-HOW

*Whether you choose classic or creative, here are some basic rules to remember when putting together any invitation.*

### Date, Time, Place, and Occasion

Always double-check that your invitation contains this information before sending it out. Convey the same information verbally if you invite your guests over the phone.

### RSVP

Let your guests know how you want them to RSVP to your event. This is especially important the larger the guest list becomes. Will it be by phone, RSVP card, or email? Keep it simple and choose only one RSVP form otherwise you're guaranteed some confusion. Also state the latest date you wish to receive RSVPs. Some hosts even go the extra mile and include a pre-stamped and addressed reply card with their invitation. This is recommended if you want your guests to RSVP with their choice of food. If this is the case, be sure to include small checkboxes on the card where guests can mark if they want meat, fish, or a vegetarian entree. Also, assign a space where they can provide any food allergies. This will make your guest list easier to organize.

### The Food

Surprises are great, but not always when it comes to food. Give a hint as to what will be served so your guests know what to expect but don't get too detailed. "Vino & Finger foods" is more than enough information for a simple cocktail party.

### Save The Date

Send out the invitations approximately three weeks before your party. Any earlier, and people may forget.

Send them any later, and the chances are that they'll already have other plans. If you're preparing a party of epic proportion that no one should miss, you can send a "Save the Date Card" six to eight weeks prior to the party to let everyone know you are planning a big event and that they should mark their calendars. Three weeks before the date, send out the real invitation.

### VIP

Write a personal note and send it along with the regular invitation if there is a person you really hope to see at your party. Not only is it a friendly gesture, but chances are he or she will be more likely to attend.

### Lists

Make one "A" and one "B" list with names. Start sending invitations to the guests on the "A" list. When you get a feel for how many can make it, start filling up with names from the "B" list. At a larger event, typically 50 percent answer "yes" on the first mailing.

### Invite Away

There are always guests that have to cancel last minute because of car trouble, illness in the family, or overtime at work. So for larger gatherings, invite one or two extra faces for every ten guests to compensate for these possible no shows. One exception to this rule is when you are hosting an intimate seated dinner party where you don't invite extra guests.

### Bring On the Boys

It's a fact: men decline invitations more often than women do. To compensate, remember to invite more men than women. That way your party will be equally mixed.

## Choose the Right Date

Get your day-planner out when picking a party date so you make sure that it doesn't coincide with a friend's birthday or any major holidays. Generally speaking, January and July are two of the worst months to plan a party; your friends are probably away on vacation in July and, let's be honest, everyone is sick of being social in January after all those Thanksgiving, Christmas, Hanukkah and New Year's celebrations.

## What Does RSVP Mean?

RSVP is short for the French expression, Réspondez s'il vous plait. Translation: please answer.

# DRESS CODE

ATTIRE INDICATES THE *party's level of elegance and puts the guests at ease so they don't have to worry about being under or overdressed for the occasion. If you suspect, however, that your guests aren't familiar with expressions like "Black Tie" and "Informal Attire," it's wise to briefly explain your dress code to avoid stress and confusion. Keep in mind that most people don't own a tuxedo with tails or a ballroom gown so people may decline your invitation if you have too many requirements. If the dress code isn't mentioned on the invitation, it's up to your guests to pick their own party outfits. A good suggestion, especially for a theme party, is to write expressions like "summer's best" on the invitation.*

### White Tie

A gala celebration! To be honest it's almost never required today unless you attend diplomatic parties or private balls.
*Him:* Black tailcoat with a white pique vest worn over a formal white shirt is required, as well as black shoes with a spit shine. White gloves on the dance floor are optional.
*Her:* A long and formal evening gown, think royalty. Gloves are perfect with this outfit and can be worn when greeting other guests and when dancing, but not when eating.

### Black Tie

Many formal events, like banquets or fundraisers, are black-tie or black-tie optional gatherings.
*Him:* A black tuxedo, white shirt, and black bow tie is the classic combination. If you decide to wear a cummberbund (totally optional—most modern tuxedos are wore without) The folds should face upward. Unless the event is totally old school, you can opt for a lighter and brighter color on the shirt, tux, and bow tie. Sometimes, you can even skip the bow tie entirely!
*Her:* A less formal long gown or shorter cocktail-length dress. Consider the time of the year and the occasion when you pick your dress. Gloves can be worn as well.

### Formal Attire

"Formal" actually means different things depending on what time the party takes place.
*Him:* Before 6:00 pm, gentlemen should wear a dark suit, with a white shirt and a traditional tie that isn't too colorful or crazy.

After 6:00 PM, formal means black-tie.
*Her:* Before 6:00 PM the lady can wear a business type of suit, a dress that isn't an evening gown, or a two-piece outfit like a skirt and a sweater. After 6:00 PM, formal means black-tie.

### Informal Attire

Be careful—informal doesn't mean casual. Again, attire depends on the time for the event.
*Him*: Before 6:00 pm, men should wear a sport coat or a suit of a preferred color, casual shirt and no tie. After 6:00 pm sport coat or a suit is still recommended, but in a darker color, with a dress shirt and tie.
*Her:* A shorter dress or dressy pants-ensemble. Before 6:00 pm, it's ok to choose a colorful outfit. After 6:00 pm, go with a darker one.

### Casual

Generally speaking, when attire is casual, this means anything goes. Shorts, sandals, and a T-shirt would be a great outfit for a casual pool party! If you want your guests to be neat, pressed, and clean you should write "dressy casual" on the invitation. This means the guests should wear something comfortable, but still a little nicer than something ordinary casual wear. "Business casual" is a term used for networking and business-related events, usually being held right after work. Opt for a crisp and neat look like something you would wear to an important meeting with your company CEO.

# GIFTS AND GOODIE BAGS

OVER THE YEARS, *it has become tradition for the host or hostess to give a small present, like a goodie-bag, when guests leave the party. Not only does it serve as a nice thank-you to your guests for coming, but it also acts as a memory of the event. Gifts can also be placed on the guests' plates as a treat, when they sit down for dinner. This way they serve as perfect icebreakers and topics of discussion around the table!*

### Home baked

Bake something indulgent your guests can eat the next morning or make your own jam or marmalade that you send along with homemade bread.

### Spa

Visit your favorite spa and tell them about your party! They might be willing to provide your party-goers with a discount card or voucher for their services. Inviting the owner to your party usually helps when trying to score some perks.

### Candy

Candy is always a great choice when it comes to gift bags. You can even take it a step further and try making your own! Handmade treats make it feel like a truly special gesture when wrapped in a cone or gift-wrapped in a box. Another idea is to buy lollipops and decorate them with self-made stickers using creative pictures or text.

### Flowers

Create small invidual fllower arrangements to use as place cards at the dinner table, then let your guests take them home at the end of the night. For your foodie friends give them planted herbs, or tulip bulbs for your gardening pals with a card explaining the plant origin.

*P.S. These gift ideas also work as excellent presents to the host or hostess — instead of that typical bottle of wine — the next time you are invited to a party yourself.*

# DÉCOR

*Delicious food, fun guests, and good music all make for a great party almost anywhere, but not in New York City. The competition is so cutthroat in the "Big Apple" that there always has to be something extraordinary about the event to attract guests. Most times, "extraordinary" means spending a lot of time and money on fantastic décor.*

*So what does it take? I've built a belvedere in Central Park, draped a penthouse completely in white for one of Jennifer Lopez's parties, rolled out a 250-foot-long lawn on Fifth Avenue and even filled a photography studio with twenty blooming cherry trees for a magazine event. With decorations like these, having a budget in the hundreds of thousands is not unusual for a major event in New York City.*

*Yet even at events like these, you'll end up in some kind of decoration crisis. Mishaps like party tents collapsing, curtains falling down, or red carpets rolling up and threatening to knock over your guests are just a few of my own décor disaster moments. Conclusion: always have your first-aid party kit and your tool-box handy! With must-haves such as a glue and staple gun, bandages, double-sided and duct tape, pins, thread, and so on, you'll be prepared for any challenge.*

# *BEFORE YOU DECORATE*

THE BEST AND *most convenient place to host a party is usually in your own apartment or home. Think about it: there's a kitchen where you can prep food, no venue fee, you know where you have everything, and you can fit more guests than you think. To maximize your available space, move big and bulky furniture to adjacent rooms that aren't being used, or store them short term with friendly neighbors you've invited.*
*With a few simple décor tips, you will quickly be able to turn your living room into a steamy tropical island, or any theme you desire. Before you can do anything, however, you need to get your space ready for the transformation…*

### ❧ *EMPTY SPACES*

Put everything that doesn't fit your party's theme, clutters up your space, or is fragile, into a closet or roped off room. This includes anything from shoes and stacks of magazines to old mail and other knick-knacks you've got laying around the house. But don't stop there! Create clean surfaces on tables, chests, windowsills, and bookshelves throughout your space to make it feel more spacious and to give guests plenty of spots to rest their drinks…on coasters of course.

### ❧ *HIDE THE VACUUM*

Use window-cleaning spray to quickly buff up shiny surfaces such as door handles, faucets, tables, and shelves. Don't worry about the dust bunnies under your sofa–no one will notice them anyway. You can give the place a deep cleaning after the party is over—there's really no need to do it twice.

### ❧ THE BATHROOM

This is the one and only room you must (and I mean must) clean thoroughly since almost every guest will need to use the facilities during the party, if even just to wash up. Scrub the sink, stock up on toilet paper and guest towels, and buy a fragrant scented candle to create a nice atmosphere. A basket with mints, scented lotion, and other toiletries will be much appreciated by all your guests throughout the night. The bathroom is also the perfect place for a flower arrangement.

### ❧ *REFURNISH*

Unless you're having a seated reception, arrange furniture—such as couches, ottomans, and armchairs—into groups with pillows and blankets to build socializing "islands" around the space. This will make your party guests more social and give the space a better "flow" for mingling.

### ❧ *TEMPORARY COAT-CHECK*

Tight on closet space? Use a curtain rod and put two chairs together, seats facing each other for balance. Place the rod on top of the chairs, add back supports, and attach the bar with tape. Put the "coat check" in a separate room.

# DECORATING

## – 5 essentials

ONCE YOU ARE *finished making all necessary preparations, it's time to decorate your venue.*
*Well-crafted and beautiful decorations enhance any event. During daytime events, focus on every small detail since it will be hard to hide defects like scuffs on the floor or scratches on the furniture. At night, these tiny problems are easily hidden with the right kind of lighting, so concentrate on creating bold, eye-catching decorations to make your space pop.*
*Five essentials when decking out your party are: fabric, color, lighting, flowers, and music. Experiment, stick to the theme, and have fun!*

 *FABRIC*

An easy way to transform any room and create a new mood is to decorate it with fabrics. You can easily have pillowcases, tablecloths, drapes or chair covers made, or whip out your needle and thread to make your own! Keep these things in mind:

 *PATTERN*

Choose a fabric with a pattern you like, one that also matches the party theme. If the event takes place in dark surroundings, go for stronger colors and bigger patterns than you normally would—otherwise they just won't pop.

 *THEME COLOR*

Pick one of the colors from your pattern of choice to serve as the party theme color . Use it when deciding on napkins, flowers, trays, cocktails and so on. This makes the party's design feel well planned and thought out.

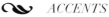 *ACCENTS*

While staying consistent with your pattern and main color scheme, dare to use totally different materials and palettes in some spots throughout the party space. This makes your design more dynamic and interesting.

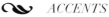 *CHEAT*

The bigger the party, the dimmer the lights and the more you can cheat with your decorations. Work your magic with glue, staple guns, and double-sided tape…after all it only has to hold up for one evening! Create new pillowcases by wrapping fabrics around your regular pillows and use a stapler to keep it in place for the night. A drapery can easily be made by using a thin pole or inexpensive curtain rod that can be adjusted into different lengths. Fold the fabric around the pole, staple it together, and hang it up. Tablecloths that match the rest of your décor are also quick and easy to make. Cut the fabric to the appropriate size, then fold in and iron the raw, un-hemmed edges. Use glue to make it stay.

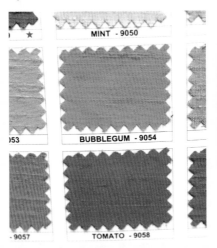

MINT - 9050

053

BUBBLEGUM - 9054

- 9057

TOMATO - 9058

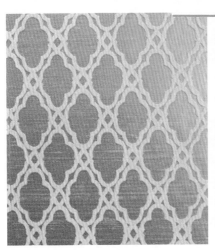

## 2. CHOICE OF COLOR

COLORS ARE SAID *to affect us subconsciously by evoking different moods. Yellow, red, and orange, for example, are said to stimulate the appetite—something many fast food restaurants have kept in mind. Before you pick your party's prominent color for fabrics, flowers, and lighting, sit down and give your options some thought.*

 WHITE
*Symbolizes:* Purity, childhood, and virginity.
*For the Party:* White makes the room feel bigger and is perfect if you want to create a neutral mood. Using only white can give your space a sterile feeling, so combine with bright pastels, silver, crystal, or gold to achieve a classy feel.

 PINK
*Symbolizes:* Sensitivity, affection, elegance, and sentimentality.
*For the Party:* Pink is very inviting and sets an atmosphere where your guests want to linger...which may not be a good idea if you want them to leave on the early side. Just be careful not to use too many bright and pastel pink colors, as this results in a very girly and adolescent look.

 ORANGE
*Symbolizes:* Happiness, optimism, self-confidence, and energy.
*For the Party:* Orange minimizes the room's size and creates a positive, vibrant, and intimate atmosphere.

RED
*Symbolizes:* Love, freedom, defiance, and chaos.
*For the Party:* Red, like orange, is vibrant and brings a lot of energy to a space. While a lighter shade of red makes a room feel more spacious, a darker hue makes it feel smaller and more decadent.

YELLOW
*Symbolizes:* Delight, happiness, independence, wisdom, and creativity.
*For the Party:* Yellow works year-round and magnifies the size of the venue. If you want a spontaneous and joyful feeling to your party, this is the color to go for.

GREEN
*Symbolizes:* Hope, balance, calm, responsibility, and success.
*For the Party:* Green is the perfect color when you want a relaxed party with quiet conversation and maybe some jazz tunes playing in the background.

BLUE
*Symbolizes:* Stability, depth, intellect, and elegance.
*For the Party:* Blue is said to help improve concentration and to have a positive effect on the brain overall. Choose blue if you want to encourage your guests to have long and intellectual conversations. Blue also gives a clean feeling to any space, which is great if you don't have time to make those door knobs squeaky clean before your party. Light blues enhance the size of the room.

BLACK
*Symbolizes:* Grief, fear, loneliness, and abandonment.
*For the Party:* You'd think that too much black would make your party a little depressing, but it's actually perfect when you're looking to bring out other strong colored objects in the design or when you want to make a room feel smaller.

## 3. LIGHTING

AN IMPORTANT AND *many times overlooked element of decorating for most parties is lighting. You can decorate all day long but if you don't light the space properly, your design just won't work! Proper illumination will make your décor look amazing, even if you cheat and put it together in a hurry.*

### ❧ OVERHEAD LIGHTS

Overhead lights are strictly forbidden during any party. The bright light they cast on your guests and space is unglamorous and definitely unflattering—not even colored light bulbs will help. Keep them turned off during the event unless they have dimmer switches.

### ❧ SPOTLIGHTS

Get inexpensive spotlights that attach with clips and direct them onto your flower arrangements, buffet, or other objects you want to highlight in the room. Use colored bulbs or heat resistant colored films or gels to achieve different moods. Colored bulbs can also be used in your ordinary lamps.

### ❧ CANDLES

Nothing creates a cozy and inviting atmosphere better than candlelight. Be generous with wax and wicks, not only on the tables but also in the windows, on trays, the floor, and preferably in clusters to maximize the effect. For safety purposes, be sure that nothing flammable is close by and attach the candle-holder to its surface with double-sided tape so it stays in place.

## Decoration Tips

- A New Room: Can you sink drawing pins to your ceiling? Congratulations! You can quickly set up a lounge area by using light fabrics hanging from the ceiling to divide up the room and placing pillows on the floor. It's a great effect and will be a popular gathering spot.
- Mirrors: Maximize the effect of your flower arrangements and candles by putting mirrors behind or underneath them. Mirrors in a narrow room create a spacious feel or make excellent serving trays. They are even a fun alternative to regular tablecloths and place-mats.
- Scents: Memories and emotions are triggered by scents. Make a spice tray with lit candles and piles of cinnamon sticks for your exotic soiree—it smells great and looks fabulous. Throwing a Christmas party? Bake gingerbread cookies just before your guests arrive to get them in a holiday mood.
- DVD: Rent a Yule log DVD for your après-ski party, summer flicks for the February indoor beach party, or a great Bollywood flick for a Bolly-inspired celebration. It will make your guests smile and enhance the party's theme.

## Outdoor Decorations

Get a glamorous feel by placing pillows, a divan, candles, and other typical indoor objects in your garden. Another outdoor-decorating tip: take branches from leafy trees and place them in buckets filled with sand or gravel. If the buckets are old and ugly, cover them with fabrics. With plenty of buckets and branches, you can create interesting outdoor rooms and shielding walls. Protect yourself against unreliable weather by renting a party tent. If the tent looks boring, simply roll up the walls and use fabric to create your own walls instead! As a budget-friendly alternative, place four tall sticks in separate sand-filled buckets and stretch a waterproof cover over the posts . If necessary, this will at least hold off a light drizzle. During dusk and evening parties, you can create beautiful effects with scattered ground torches or lanterns in the trees.

## Smoking

Decide what your rules will be for smoking before the party kicks off. Should the guests go outside, or are they allowed to smoke inside in a restricted area? (For example, next to a window.) Even if you are against smoking, make sure the smoking area is nicely decorated and has visible ashtrays, preferably tall ones, to mark the spot. Regular flowerpots turned upside down on a plate do the trick.

## Spruce Up Your Wall

Bored with your plain, white walls?, Spruce them up with a little color simply by up-lighting them using colored spotlights! If you're feeling really creative, why not buy large cheap canvases and spray-paint them with a color or cover with a fabric? Hang them in place of your own pictures on the walls in order to protect your art and to tie in the theme.

## Candle Wax

Don't worry about wax spills when decorating with candles. Just freeze it the next day with ice, and then easily remove it.

## Design Your Own Candles

Search online or in magazines for images that fit the party's theme. Copy and cut to size, and tape the pictures around regular drinking glasses then place tea light candles inside.

## 4. FLOWER ARRANGEMENTS

FLOWERS ALWAYS BRING *a wonderful feel to parties, especially during intimate, daytime gatherings where they are easy to spot. During nighttime events, light your floral creations with simple spotlights as they will otherwise "disappear" in the darkness and no one will see your artistic abilities. Is your party a sit-down event, like a dinner or a standing affair, like a cocktail party? In either situation, adjust the placement of your arrangements so that they rest at eye level. When selecting flowers, don't always choose the ones you think are the prettiest. Instead, look at the whole picture and pick the types that complement each other and suit the party theme. Always include one or two plump flowers that give a lot of color, one type that hangs down if you want to cover the vase, and twigs and grass to create volume and height.*

*Be careful that you don't mix too many exotic flowers in any one arrangement, since they tend to be quite difficult to match. Also, show consideration to allergy sufferers by going light on strongly scented flowers.*

### HOW TO MAKE YOUR OWN FLOWER ARRANGEMENT

❧ Clean the flower stems as soon as youget home—leaves quickly rot in water and create bacteria. Next, cut flower stems diagonally so they drink water better. With bushes and twigs, cut a cross in their trunks.

❧ Put the flowers in water a couple of hours before arranging them so they have time to open up. If not, you risk the chance that they will open up later and alter the shape of your design. If you're in a rush, use lukewarm water to make the flowers open up more quickly.

❧ Use wet oasis in the base of the vase instead of water to shape the arrangement easily. Fewer spills are, of course, an added bonus.

❧ If you are using a water-filled vase, tape a checked pattern on the vase's opening. This will help you spread the flowers evenly as you arrange.

❧ Place the vase at eye level when creating your arrangement. Shape a round and even form to look like half a ball. Rotate the vase to make sure your designis how you want it to look from each and every angle. Don't forget to look at the form underneath to make sure the edge is even.

❧ Not every host wants their flower arrangements take the shape of a half ball so don't be afraid to experiment with different heights and shapes. You can also mix in other materials such as feathers, straws of reed, sparkling spray, and much more.

❧ When you're done, place the flowers in a cool spot to maintain freshness and help them keep their shape until the party starts.

## GREAT PARTY FLOWERS

### PEONIES

An evening party favorite with its grand and colorful petals. Just a few are enough to make the arrangement plump, magnificent and fragrant. Can be found in a variety of different colors.

### RANUNCULUS

Colorful, but more petite and fragile then peonies. Perfect for a daytime event.

### ROSES

The classic of classics. Roses can be used in many different ways. Put on your gardening gloves and run your hand alongside the stems to get rid of any thorns before arranging them—the last thing you want is for one of your guests to prick their hand!

### TULIPS

They are always "in" and can be found in every color imaginable. A great choice for parties that take place during the day.

### CARNATIONS

Carnations, though not the most popular, are ideal when making creative forms. They offer a less expensive way to use flowers of any color, and stay fresh for quite some time. The drawback is that they are difficult to match with other flowers, and are usually best used on their own.

### LILLIES

Dramatic and great for an evening party. Remove the pollen pastilles before you arrange them so that guests don't get painted in yellow when they smell the beautiful flora. Be careful with heavily scented varieties like Casablanca. Guests may react negatively to the strong fragrance.

### TWIGS AND LEAVES

Gives beautiful height and a creative, festive, and striking look to your arrangements. Buy or pick your own twigs, add a few tulips, and voila! You have a super easy and pretty spring arrangement. Leaves give a splendid array of color to your fall arrangements

## Flower Hearts and Disco Balls

Want to make an arrangement out of the ordinary? Cut dry oasis into the outline you want. Wrap the oasis in chicken wire before wetting it and sticking flowers into it. The wire makes sure that the ceiling hanging arrangement keeps its shape and doesn't fall apart onto the heads of admiring guests.

## Oasis

Oasis is a condensed foam that is used to arrange flowers. With it, you can easily achieve desired shapes and heights for your arrangements, and it couldn't be easier to use! Soak the oasis for at least 30 minutes before adding the flowers. No additional water is needed. Buy oasis at your local florist.

## Budget Tips

To save on vases, use every day water glasses of different shapes, sizes, and colors. Cover their insides with leaves, or their outside with colored paper to achieve your desired effect.

You don't always have to use expensive cut flowers from the florist when decorating your party. Potted plants in regular clean, simple and colorful pots are a less expensive alternative that look great at any party. Hyacinths and azaleas are popular potted plants and work well as decoration.

## The Restroom

You should always put flowers in the restroom to make it more attractive and more inviting.

## At the Dinner Table

Tall arrangements are great, but not on the dining table. Make low compositions so the guests can see each other from opposite sides of the table. A single flower handpicked in your garden, or a few smaller flowers arranged in mini bouquets at each plate give a warm and welcoming feel to the table.

## Quantity, Please

Just like candles, several bouquets grouped together can make a striking presentation. Vary size and height, but remember to keep a consistent color theme with the flowers.

## Tape

Attach vases with double-sided tape to the surface they're on. This will prevent the arrangement from falling in the unlikely event someone bumps into it.

## Variation

Don't dwell on making all of your arrangements look exactly the same. Variation makes the room more interesting! Just stick to a theme, like a color or a specific flower that is found in each arrangement. Using the same flower, but in a variety of different vases clustered together, is simple but striking.

## Clear Vases

These vases are inexpensive and can be found in a variety of shapes and sizes. One downside, however, is that the stems and oasis show through and can be difficult to cover if the vase is tall.

## Tip!

Big leaves on the inside of the vase give a great effect while hiding ugly stalks. Give your vases a different look that goes with your theme by using leaves in new shapes or colors.

## Call the Florist

Flowers are seasonal and this can affect their price. Tulips, for example, are more expensive in the winter than they are during the spring. To get a better idea of what's in season, pick up the phone and ask your local florist in order to find the best prices. As always, be courteous and give your florist fair warning if you want a large number of a certain flower. This way, he/she can be sure to have them in stock when you'll need them.

## 5. PARTY MUSIC

Great music does wonders for a party. It fills the room with energy and reinforces the party's theme. Music also helps the guests to relax and feel at ease. Moral of the story: always play music! Even when you're hosting a sit down dinner, you should have some music on in the background for ambiance—just go easy on the volume. Your guests should still be able to talk to one other without straining to hear. In order to avoid rushing to the stereo and changing tracks every three minutes, create your own playlist to play on your computer or iPod. You should always choose tunes you enjoy yourself, but be considerate of your guests. If you are a huge fan of heavy metal, feel free to include a few of your favorite tracks, but mix it up with songs appealing to a wider audience. If you find yourself all alone on the dance floor, it's probably a good indication that you should consider playing something else.

If you can't play from your computer or if you don't have an MP3 player, head to your local record store and check out the movie soundtrack section. Soundtracks are written to evoke a certain mood and usually stick to a single theme for more than an hour. Choose a record that suits your party. Playlists and soundtracks are great, but nothing beats a live band, if your budget allows. Even the dullest holiday party will rock if a live group can go on stage and play some classic covers or festive hits.

# THE VENUE

SOMETIME IT'S NECESSARY *to throw the party outside your home, either for practical reasons or because you just really want to try a new environment. Parties at venues can be extremely expensive if you settle on an old mansion or a French chateau, but there are also plenty of inexpensive, but still fabulous, alternatives.*

### The Art Gallery
These funky premises always have great lighting, and it's a win-win situation. Not only do you get a fun venue for your party, but the gallery owner also gets to showcase his art for potential buyers. For this reason, you can ask to use the gallery for free or for a discounted price. Perfect for a larger cocktail party with twenty-five guests or more.

### The Spa or Shop
Maybe your favorite spa or shop can stay open a few extra hours for a night? While you're there, perhaps they can give you and your guests a great discount on purchases made during the event. While they get great PR, your guests get a bargain, and you get a new venue.. Perfect for a fun and relaxing night out!

### The Miniature Golf Course
Book the whole course for you and your friends. Make it an early-bird event, and chances are you'll get a great deal. Bring some music and golf your way around the course while everyone (everyone of le-gal age, that is) sips on drinks. Perfect for all ages.

### The Night Club
Bars and night clubs want guests and are usually willing to rent their spaces for a good price, or even for free since they stand to make a profit on the food and alcohol sales. Have the party in the middle of the week and it will be easier to find a bargain. Always negotiate on everything, even the alcohol. If you don't rent out the entire space, make sure you at least get your own VIP room or section. It's more exciting if you decide on a place that recently opened but be sure to scout the location first though. Bars and night clubs are perfect venues if you have a lot of guests but not a lot of money.

### In the Open
If you trust your luck against the weather, your possibilities are endless. You can host amazing parties on the beach, by the pool, in a park, by the garden, on a ski slope, and so on.

# TABLE SETTING

*O*ne of the most intricate table settings I designed was for an event hosted by Food Network and Home and Garden Television. It took place on the ninety-eighth-floor penthouse in one of Donald Trump's skyscrapers. The enormous apartment was raw, and we decorated it from scratch to make it look like a glamorous home for one night only. We ended up renting antique furniture, parts of TV sets, and even books by the yard. Imagine getting all that up to the ninety-eighth-floor! I collaborated with TV hosts from the network on the interior, and with Rachel Ray, Emeril, Bobby Flay, and the other Food Network stars on what food should be served. One of the HGTV hosts had seen gorgeous green granite plates that she just had to have for the party. My task was to find 150 of them, and after a long search I finally found them in California. Not only did they cost a small fortune, but we also had to ship them ex- press via truck across the country to NYC. But in the end, it was worth it. They looked fantastic on the dinner table!

For a luxury jewelry-brand dinner, I had almost a thousand white roses sprayed with the company's logo in gold. The arrangement was stunning, and I was asked to do a feature story in Brides magazine about how to monogram everything from spoons to leaves with Swarovski crystals.

# HOW TO SET YOUR TABLE

*DON'T PANIC IF you don't have enough place settings to accommodate all your guests. Even if you're missing a plate here or a bowl there, it's trendy to mix and match vintage china and other pieces for a striking effect (it's also a much more appealing alternative than paper and plastic). To ensure your set-up doesn't look too cluttered, use single-colored pieces to anchor each setting, for example, all-white chargers.*

*Vintage pieces look beautiful, but you don't want to risk smashing your grandmother's antique soup tureen during a dinner party. As an alternative, you can always rent china to use in place of pieces that hold a special place in your heart.*

*It's a fact: things break and get dirty at every party. Therefore, always have back-up plates, tablecloths, cutlery, and anything else guests might need. Always have extra glasses: 25% extra for a dinner party, and at least 100% extra glassware for a cocktail party.*

### ❧ THE DINNER PLATE
Place the plate approximately one inch from the table's edge. This rule can be tricky to follow if you have a round table. so don't worry if it isn't perfect.

### ❧ THE CHARGER
If you are hosting a fancy dinner, you should place a large decorative charger plate on the table as a base. On top of the charger, place the plates for the starter and main course. Remove it before serving dessert.

### ❧ THE BREAD PLATE
This is a small plate, placed to the side and used for serving bread. The butter knife should be laid horizontally across the plate, and remember to place butter on the table before the guests arrive. If the table is small, this is the first plate to go.

### ❧ NAPKINS
You can place the napkins wherever you like. On top of the dinner plates, next to the cutlery, or even on the chair backs. Be creative.

### ❧ GLASSES
During dinner it's common to use several different glasses: one glass for white wine, one for red, and one for water. Place your glasses above the dinner plate, slightly to the right, since most guests are right handed.

The glasses should be placed in the order in which they will be used, with the first glass to be used placed to the left of the water glass.

### ❧ FORKS
If you want to set your table Americana style, place the forks to the left of the plate with the prongs facing upwards. Flip the forks over, so the prongs face into the table, and voila—you've made it a French setting. When using numerous forks, place the one that the guest should start with to the far left. A starter fork should be smaller than the fork used for the main course.

A proper host should never place more than three forks next to the plate (not counting the dessert fork, placed above the plate). If you needs more forks, bring them to the table when are needed. There are, however, exceptions such as at grand affairs with lots of guests. In this case, it's best to have all the forks on the table from the start to make dinner run as smoothly as possible, even if there are more than three.

### ❧ KNIVES
Place your knifes to the right of the plate. When using more than one knife, put the first one to be used to the far right. The knives' edges should always face the plate.

This rule also goes for butter knives. As with forks, the starter knife should be smaller than the ones used for the main course. Correct etiquette is to never set the table with more than two knives next to the plate, not counting the butter knife. If more than two knives are needed, bring them in just before they are needed. At big events, it is okay to cheat and have more than two knives on the table from the start to make serving easier.

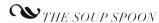

### THE SOUP SPOON

Place the spoon to the far right, outside the knives.

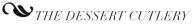

### THE DESSERT CUTLERY

Proper etiquette is to set the table with both a dessert spoon and dessert fork that are placed on the table before the meal, just above the plate. If you experience a cutlery shortage choose the ones you have the most of.

### THE COFFEE SET

At larger dinners, save time by placing coffee cups on the table before the meal. Set it behind the water glass so it's not in the way during the meal and lay the spoon on the plate to the right. Milk and sugar are put on the table when dessert is being served. A nice alternative is to bring out the cups just before the dessert course using trays prepared in advance with cups, milk, and sugar to make the transition as easy as possible.

## Asian Table Setting

Use bowls instead of plates, and chopsticks instead of cutlery. If you place the chopsticks directly on the table you have a Chinese setting. By placing the tip of the sticks onto a little stone, or ceramic cube, you have a Japanese setting. Place everything on a low table so you can sit on pillows instead of chairs.

## When Accidents Happen

At the website www.replacementsltd.com you can find parts for your set if anything breaks. The site has a large selection. Some plates, glasses, and cutlery are more than 100 years old!

## Table Manners

There really is no elegant or easy way to correct someone's manners. The best way is to set a good example for your guests. Here are some tips:

– Don't bring anything extra to the table, like a half full cocktail glass, cigarettes, or unfinished canapés. For men, keep belongings like cameras off of the table, for women, hang your handbag on the back of your chair or on the floor under your chair.
– Put the napkin in your lap and leave it there throughout dinner. A napkin isn't a handkerchief, so don't blow your nose in it! If you have to leave the table, place the napkin on the seat until you return.
– When you're finished eating, place the knife and fork together as if the plate was a clock, and the utensils are the hands showing twenty minutes past four. If you just need to take a short break, you place them twenty minutes before four. Never put used utensils on the tablecloth. When you're finished eating, feel free to put the napkin on the table.
– Don't salt and pepper your food until you've tasted it first.
– Eat European style by placing the food on the rounded backside of the fork. It's considered quite posh.

Eating American style by using the ladled front of the fork is many times easier.

When Accidents Happen
You can usually find replacement parts if anything breaks at www.replacementsltd.com. The site has a large selection. Some plates, glasses, and cutlery are more than 100 years old!
– Don't cut all your meat or fish at once. Two pieces at the same time is more than enough.
– Feel free to lean your forearms on the table's edge but please—no elbows on the table.
– Never pick your teeth at the table. Not even if you try to hide the act with your hand or a napkin.
– Stay calm even if someone spills on your best tablecloth. First, ensure the guest that it doesn't matter (even if it does) and then clean up as much possible. Don't use fabrics and dining sets that can't handle a spill or a crack. Almost every party has a few accidents.
– Take one sip at a time from your drink or wine—no gulping!
– When drinking white wine, hold the glass by the stem to keep it colder, longer. While enjoying red wine, served room temperature, hold the bowl of the glass.

# NAPKINS

A NICELY FOLDED *napkin is an easy way to enhance the general look of your table setting. Fabric napkins are preferable. If you don't have any, you can easily sew some up or find someone who can do it for you. Since you won't need much yardage, treat yourself to a fabric of high quality such as silk or linen. Standard napkin sizes are twelve, fourteen, and sixteen square inches. In the long run, it's always cheaper to use cloth napkins, which you can have cleaned, and disposable paper napkins, which get thrown away after one use.*

*Napkins can be more than just pretty—use them to hold a menu, small gift, or even a beautiful flower.*

*IDEAS FOR NAPKIN FOLDS
(see opposite page)*

1. A practical and simple fold for the buffet. Attach a ribbon around the napkin and put the cutlery underneath it.

2. An ordinary fold becomes extraordinary when you experiment with different materials. This napkin has a leaf instead of a fabric strap and a brooch to hold it in place.

3. For the fancy dinner you can place the menu in the napkins. This will give your guests something to talk about.

4. Buy wax from a stationery store and use it to spruce up old or thicker paper napkins.

5. Look through drawers and cupboards to find things to decorate with. Tufts, dried flowers, bookmarks, rhinestones…if you can find it, you can use it.

6. Turn your napkin into a seating card.

## Linen Facts

If you have old beautiful linen napkins and tablecloths, use them! It won't hurt them, and it's better then just letting them lay in the cupboard, waiting for to be eaten by moths.

Here is some general advice on how to keep your linens fresh:

– Never put anything but completely clean and stain-free napkins back into the cupboard or drawer. Even washed stains will attract moths.

– New linen is washed in 140°F water for as short a time as possible. Never tumble dry. Go for a perborate and brightener-free detergent.

– To brighten and clean old linens, put them in room temperature water overnight, then wash by hand. Roll the linen in towels to remove excessive water and let air dry.

– Linen is best when it's allowed to dry outside, but avoid drying in direct sunlight.

– Roll up napkins or press them flat. Don't hot iron them over their folds since this will make them fragile.

– Keep them in a dark cupboard with a few bags of dried lavender to keep them smelling fresh.

# TABLECLOTHS

FEEL FREE TO *skip the tablecloth when having a party. If you have a beautiful tabletop, show it off and use colorful placemats to add interest to the table. Picture frames and mirrors can also work as alternatives to a tablecloth, however many do prefer setting a table with fabric. Warm-colored and patterned tablecloths add a welcoming feel, while the classic white cloth gives a clean, stark look. Reflect over what your table should look like to fit your theme before choosing.*

*A good thing about tablecloths is that they protect your tabletops from stains and scratches or cover existing ones. They are also good at minimizing the sharp "cling" and "clang" from glasses and silverware being moved during the party.*

*There isn't a rule for how long a tablecloth should be, so simply use your best judgement when picking out the right one. Keep in mind that the fabric needs at least ten inches on all four sides to get a beautiful drop—a thirty-inch drop is pretty standard. To find your size, measure the table's length and width. If you want ten inches of drop you add on twenty inches to both the length and width before measuring out your fabric. When using a round table, simply measure the diameter.*

### Placemats

Want to set your table with placemats but don't have any? Use what you can find. Colorful and fun patterned cloth napkins act as perfect placemats as do picture frames, cutting boards, graphic trays, and even banana leaves. Don't be afraid to get creative!

## Design Your Tablecloth

Got a great tablecloth or a piece of fabric you love, but it's not big enough to cover the whole table? Use it anyway. Start by laying a discreetly colored fabric in the correct length as your base, then layer the decorative cloth on top.

## Box the Table

Long tablecloths that go all the way down to the floor will have extra fabric wrinkled up in the corners. Box the table if you want a more austere silhouette.

1. Take the overflowing fabric hanging in the corner and stretch it out into a wing, so the creases even out.
2. Pull the wing diagonally to the rear.
3. Place your hand on the middle of the wing and fold it in under the tablecloth that is lying flat on the table.
4. Even out and make adjustments with pins, if necessary.

Tip! By boxing a regular white sheet you quickly get a classic-looking tablecloth, and no one will ever know the difference.

## Guests & Tablecloth Chart

How many guests can I fit around a 60-inch round table? This chart will tell you. It also provides you with tablecloth sizes for a 30-inch drop.

| Round Tables: | Seats | Max | Tablecloth |
| --- | --- | --- | --- |
| 30″ | 2 | 4 | 90″ diameter |
| 36″ | 4 | 5 | 96″ |
| 48″ | 6 | 8 | 108″ |
| 54″ | 7 | 9 | 114″ |
| 60″ | 8 | 10 | 120″ |
| 66″ | 9 | 11 | 126″ |
| 72″ | 10 | 12 | 132 ″ |

| Square Tables: | Seats | Max | Tablecloth: |
| --- | --- | --- | --- |
| 36″ x 36″ | 4 | 6 | 96″ x 96″ |
| 48″ x 48″ | 6 | 8 | 108″ x108″ |
| 60″ x 60″ | 8 | 10 | 120″ x 120″ |
| 72″ x 72″ | 10 | 12 | 132″ x 132″ |

| Rect. Tables: | Seats | Max | Tablecloth: |
| --- | --- | --- | --- |
| 6′ x 36″ | 8 | 8 | 132″ x 96″ |
| 6′ x 42″ | 8 | 10 | 132″ x 102″ |
| 8′ x 36″ | 10 | 10 | 156″ x 96″ |
| 8′ x 42″ | 10 | 12 | 156″ x 102″ |

# TABLE SEATING

WHEN YOU HAVE *ten or more guests gathered for dinner, it's nice to assign seats. It makes the table more dynamic, and with a little thought from you, guests end up next to dining partners they share common interests with. Most hosts break into hot flashes as soon as they hear the word seating chart but relax—it's not a life or death matter, nor is it rocket science. There are three simple rules to keep in mind when you seat guests for a regular dinner party:*

1. Guests should be seated, alternating men and women by seat.
2. Each gentleman's lady is seated to his left.
3. Couples are never each other's partners, unless it's their wedding.

The rest is common sense. Try not to seat a hunter next to a passionate vegan, unless you believe that heated discussions are the way to create a memorable dinner pary.

Always wait until the day before the party to compose your seating, so possible last-minute changes on the guest list are included.

To make planning easier, draw a seating chart of all your tables on a paper and number them. If possible, laminate the sheet. Write down your guest's name on stickers, one color for the ladies and another for the gents. The laminated surface will make it easier to move the stickers around if and when you change your mind

during the process or want to try different arrangements.

If you have a large group of guests, it's a good idea to set up a separate table at your party where you place the name cards from A–Z. Pin a silk ribbon over the cards so they stay put. On each name card, designate the guest's table number, so he or she can easily find their table. Frame the table numbers, and place them on each table. Then, place cards at each seat, indicating where the guest is sitting. Round tables are beautiful, but keep in mind that they take up more space and don't seat as many guests as rectangular or square tables do. Also remember to make every guest feel included at the party. If you invite someone last minute due to cancellations, make sure that person gets a good seat where he or she feels warmly welcomed. Here are some shortcuts if you're still having issues with your seating arrangements:

### *SEATING SHORTCUT 1*

#### Number the Tables

If you have more then two tables, number them and divide the guests into equal groups. Put individuals you believe will get along well in the same group, but try to avoid good friends and couples at the same table; they will likely spend most of their time talking to each other. Spread the storytellers evenly around the room. Arrange a name card table assigning table numbers and let the guests seat themselves. To seat your guests male, female, male, you can use colored napkins, cards that say "Reserved for a Lady," or gifts at each plate that differ for men and women.

### *SEATING SHORTCUT 2*

#### Random

If you don't have the time, or energy, to think about seating, you can always let chance decide. Try using a deck of cards! If you've invited twenty people, draw ten cards and divide each card into two halves. Ladies and gents that draw the same card sit next to each other at the table. When the number of guests is uneven, you become the joker with a predetermined seat.

## Seats

Just a few chairs are enough at a cocktail party since the idea is that guests should stroll around and mingle. At a bigger buffet party, approximately 50% of the guests should be able to sit down. For a brunch, smaller buffet, tea party, or dinner gathering, you'll need seats for each and every guest.

## The Twenty-Inch Rule

Each guest should have at least twenty inches of "private" table space from left to right when sitting down. Are you having parallel tables where the guest has a neighbor behind her? The free space between the backs of the chairs when both guests are seated should be twenty inches as well. This distance is necessary if anyone needs to leave the table.

## Place Markers

Instead of traditional place cards, experiment with unique place markers. Write on driftwood, shells, jam jars, cards attached to roses, glasses that the guests can take home with them, or on cookies using frosting. If the party has a traditional or formal invitation, the place markers should always match the paper and design.

## Weddings

Seating at weddings differs greatly from a regular party. Many times, a head table is used for the bride, groom and sometimes other guests of honor.

– The bride and the groom are always seated in the middle of the wedding's head table with the bride sitting to her groom's left.
– The bride's father sits to her left. To his left is the mother of the bride.
– The groom's mother sits to his right. To her right is the groom's father.
– The best man sits at the head of the table on the bride's side. On the groom's side is the maid of honor.
– Guests closely related to the bride and groom should be seated nearest the head table.
– If parents have been divorced and remarried, it's a good idea to invite some of their relatives and seat them at that table closest to the head table.
– Many find these head table arrangements very sensitive and tricky. A good alternative is the so-called "Sweetheart Table," where only the bride and groom are seated. This is a good way to avoid all the drama.

# *BAR*

*S*ome people have very expensive taste—even when it comes to cocktails. The most expensive drink I've ever tried: The "You're Hired!," a drink offered at Donald Trump's World Bar, which I got to try when I attended a party for his TV show The Apprentice. Mixed with cognac from the days of Napoleon, black raspberry liqueur, and grape vodka, this pricy drink costs one thousand dollars. There was also the "You're Fired" cocktail available, which cost less than ten bucks.

While the "You're Hired!" may be one of my best cocktail experiences, my worst is from a party I put together for a high-end photography magazine. Going into the event, I was so proud of my new martini recipe—made from pomegranate and black grape juice. While it was being passed around I noticed that guests started to stick their tongues out at each other, and that both their teeth and tongues had turned black. Oops! At the time, there was nothing else to do but play dumb and hide in the kitchen while the drink continued to be passed around. Needless to say, my guests didn't smile much for the photographers that evening, but at least the drink was delicious.

# COCKTAILS

ALWAYS MAKE SURE *your guests are greeted with a drink when they enter the party as it will put them at ease and give them something to do with their hands. A drink also works as a great ice-breaker between guests at a party. Using a cocktail shaker to mix each and every drink by hand looks fantastic, but if you don't have a professional bartender on hand it can take forever and get rather messy. As an alternative, pitchers of premixed cocktails or serving a punch allow you to quickly pour multiple drinks without spilling and also allows you to control the alcohol content—great for any budget. The most important thing to keep in mind? Always, always, always have a non-alcoholic drink alternative on hand.*

## THE DO-IT-YOURSELF BAR

If balancing fancy trays around all night isn't for you, then the self-help bar is a great alternative. Let your guests do the work for you and look stylish as they shake their own cocktails behind the bar, socializing with one another all the while. Before any party, use this guide when stocking your DIY bar:

### TABLE
Choose a table that's long and skinny. 6 or 8 ft by 30 or 36 inches wide is usually good.

### LOCATION
Place the table in a spot where there is room for people to gather. Make sure it's easily accessible since there will be a lot of "refill traffic" going on throughout the night.

### ALCOHOL
Place alcohol bottles on trays, and put the trays in the middle of the table. This way, bottles can be reached from many different angles at the same time.

### MIXERS & ICE
Double up on all of your mixers and place them, with the ice, on both sides of the alcohol. These will be your two mixing stations. Place your cocktail shakers and other various bar tools here as well.

### GARNISHES
Cherries, pickled onions, lime and lemon wedges, straws, and other garnishes that guests can add to their drinks should be placed in decorative containers next to the mixers and ice.

### GLASSES & NAPKINS
Put the glasses on trays and cocktail napkins on plates at the table's edge where they can be easily reached.

### COCKTAIL RECIPES
Find or create recipes that use alcohol and mixers you are serving at your do-it-yourself bar. Write down or print the recipes and place them in frames on the table so that guests can be their own bartenders. You can also leave out a bartenders guide at the bar for guests who may need a little extra help.

# A COMPLETE BAR

*What makes a bar complete? The "Big 7," that's what. Any "full" bar should include the following seven alcohols: vodka, gin, rum, tequila, whiskey, brandy, and liqueur.*
*Building a full bar from scratch can be very expensive and when it is finally complete do you really want to serve your rare cognac at 2 AM anyway? A more cost-effective alternative for parties is to serve a bar with one type of spirit (for example, flavored vodka bar). Before the party, put berries, spices, fruit or whatever is in season in vodka and let it soak for at least a couple of days. Before using the vodka, strain to remove any remnants and serve in shot glasses on a bed of ice. Rum, gin, and tequila are other popular "one spirit" bars.*

*"THE BIG 7"*

**Vodka** – Most vodka is produced from grain, but can also be made from potatoes. Usually the alcohol is strained through charcoal to extract impurities and produce a beverage as tasteless and as smooth as possible. Vodka from Eastern Europe has an oily texture and sweet taste, while Finnish vodka is considered to be the most pure.

**Gin** – A distinctly flavored dry spirit that derives its character from juniper berries, as well as hints of coriander and citrus. Gin is believed to have been invented in Holland sometime during the 17th century when it was sold in chemist stores for good health. During the Thirty Years' War, British soldiers brought the spirit back home and called it "Dutch courage." Dry gin is the most common type seen today, but there is also a sweet version, called Old Tom, which is used when mixing a Tom Collins—one of many classic cocktails..

**Liqueur** – A sweet, flavored spirit originally composed to camouflage poor tasting alcohol. During the 14th century people, believed that liqueur, made from vodka and flavored with honey and herbs, protected against the Plague. Of course, the mixture didn't work (26 million Europeans died) but that didn't stop them from drinking it. Liqueurs comes in all different strengths and flavors from coffee, almond and chocolate to fruit flavors like orange, peach and cherry.

**Rum** – The world's most common spirit. Rum originates from the West Indies but is produced today wherever sugar cane grows. There are two main rum varieties: Rhum Agricole, which is made exclusively using sugar cane juice, and Rhum Industrial, which is made using molasses. The molasses rums generally have a neutral taste and are in most cases translucent. Many rums are distilled with spices to achieve characteristic flavor profiles.

**Tequila** – Hundreds of years ago, the Aztec Indians of Latin America enjoyed a fermented beverage made with sap from the agave plant. They called this beverage "pulque." When the Spaniards arrived, they brought with them the art of distillation which they used to experiment with the blue agave plant once their sherry supplies ran dry. Their quest to produce a spirit out of the plant succeeded in the town of Tequila, and to this day tequila can only be produced in this area. Silver and gold tequilas are not aged. Reposado is aged a minimum of two months, but less than a year in oak barrels, and añejo is aged between one and three years. It's a common misunderstanding that tequila is made using sap from a cactus when, in reality, the agave plant is actually an amaryllis. Mezcal resembles tequila but has more of a smoky taste and is produced all over Mexico with many different types of agave. Mezcal usually contains a signature "worm" or larvae at the bottom—so please, sip slowly.

**Whiskey** – Produced worldwide with different regional characteristics, Irish whiskey is primarily made from barley and wheat. The mash is dried over coal to get a smooth flavor, while its Scottish cousin is dried over peat, which gives it a distinct smoky flavor. What the two countries have in common is that they both age the whiskey in oak barrels for at least three years. Bourbon is the most famous American whiskey, and its main ingredient is corn. Rather than being aged in plain oak barrels, bourbon is aged in burnt oak barrels for a minimum of two years. This is where its burnt flavor and hint of vanilla comes from.

**Brandy** – Distilled wine that has been aged in oak barrels. Cognac, the most famous brandy, is produced in a French region known by the same name. To know how long a cognac has been aged you have to decode the label. VS or *** means 2 years; VSOP or VO, 5 years; and XO or Napoléon, 6 years. These are minimum aging requirements. Most of the time, however, cognac has been aged even longer.

## ∾ Ice

approximately one pound of ice per person to have enough for both drinks and possible ice baths. Ice baths are the best way to cool beverages, like beer and wine, if you are having a bigger party. To create one, simply fill a tub half way with ice, and about 1/8 of the way with water. Add bottles, and leave them to cool in the bath for approximately thirty minutes or until they have reached desired temperature. A second, and perhaps underused technique: Lplace  bottles in your washing machine and cover them with ice. As the ice melts, the water will go straight down the drain, and at the end of the evening you won't have to lift and empty heavy tubs. If you want to show off a little bit you can make your own specialty ice cubes that match your party's theme. Make cubes out of orange juice, or put berry's or small flowers in the tray before adding water. Ice actually adds flavor to a drink so make sure you're using clean, filtered water when making cubes from scratch. Ice cubes are used in cocktails since they melt slowly whereas crushed ice is used only for frozen or blended drinks.

## ∾ Fruit

Works both as a decoration and flavor enhancer. High-quality alcohol brands can be expensive so get the cheap stuff for your next mixed-drink party and simply use high-end freshly squeezed juices and homemade fruit purées to mask the flavor. You'll save some dough without skimping on the flavor. Don't be afraid to experiment using exotic fruits for your drinks.

## ∾ Tools

Indispensable, must-have bar tools including the following: a tall cocktail spoon to stir drinks, a shaker, cocktail strainer, a small paring knife to cut fruit, a small cutting board, tongs for fruit and ice, a wine opener, and finally, a bottle opener (preferably with a spiked tip for opening juice cans as well).

Liquor & Mixers Quantity Chart for Full Bar

| Guests | 10-25 | 25-35 | 35-60 | 60-100 |
|---|---|---|---|---|
| *The Spirits (bottles)* | | | | |
| White wine | 7 | 7 | 8 | 11 |
| Red wine | 2 | 3 | 5 | 6 |
| Champagne | 4 | 5 | 6 | 6 |
| Vermouth, dry | 1 | 1 | 2 | 2 |
| Vermouth, red | 1 | 1 | 1 | 1 |
| Vodka | 3 | 3 | 3 | 4 |
| Rum | 2 | 2 | 2 | 2 |
| Gin | 1 | 2 | 2 | 3 |
| Scotch | 1 | 2 | 2 | 3 |
| Whiskey | 2 | 2 | 3 | 4 |
| Bourbon | 1 | 1 | 1 | 1 |
| Tequila | 2 | 2 | 2 | 3 |
| Brandy/Cognac | 1 | 2 | 2 | 3 |
| Apertif | 1 | 1 | 2 | 3 |
| Cordial | 2 | 2 | 2 | 3 |
| Beer (bottles/cans) | 50 | 75 | 80 | 100 |
| *The Mixers (2-liter bottles)* | | | | |
| Club soda/seltzer | 3 | 3 | 4 | 5 |
| Ginger ale | 2 | 2 | 2 | 3 |
| Cola | 3 | 3 | 3 | 4 |
| Diet cola | 3 | 3 | 3 | 4 |
| Lemon-lime soda | 2 | 3 | 3 | 4 |
| Tonic | 2 | 2 | 3 | 3 |
| *Juice (quarts)* | | | | |
| Tomato | 2 | 2 | 3 | 3 |
| Grapefruit | 2 | 2 | 3 | 3 |
| Orange | 2 | 2 | 3 | 3 |
| Cranberry | 2 | 2 | 3 | 3 |
| *Extras* | | | | |
| Grenadine | 1 | 1 | 1 | 2 |
| Angostura | 1 | 1 | 1 | 2 |

# CLASSIC COCKTAILS

THERE ARE ALWAYS *new seasons and trends in cocktails. However, these recipes have been around for decades and are always popular at a party. Guests love them but surprisingly many times have never tried them.*

## 1 SIDE CAR

1 oz brandy or congac
1 oz Cointreau
1 oz fresh lemon juice

*My personal favorite to serve at a classic cocktail party.*

1. Burn an orange peel over a cocktail glass to extract a strong citrus flavor. (See p. 71) Save the peel to use for garnish.
2. Shake all the ingredients, over ice, in a cocktail shaker and strain the mixture into the cocktail glass.
3. Garnish with the orange peel.

## 2 MODERN TOM COLLINS

1½ oz gin
1 oz fresh lemon juice
1 oz simple syrup
Club soda
Cherry, and an orange
   slice for garnish

*The original drink was so popular at the turn of the century that a special Collins glass was made just for it. Sweet gin was used for a time, but now regular gin is commonly used.*

1. Combine gin, lemon juice, and simple syrup over ice in a cocktail shaker. Strain over a highball glass filled with ice.
2. Top off with club soda.
3. Garnish with the cherry and orange slice.

> ### Simple Syrup
>
> Mix equal parts water and sugar in a saucepan. Stir over medium heat until all of the sugar has dissolved. Perfect for sweetening ice-cold drinks, and guaranteed sugar lump free.

## 3 COSMOPOLITAN

1½ oz citron vodka
¾ oz Cointreau or Triple
   sec
1 oz cranberry juice
½ oz fresh lime juice
Burnt orange peel

*A modern classic that hit the scene when Absolut Citron was launched and became world famous with help from the TV series Sex and the City. Can be served " straight-up" (without ice) as well as "on the rocks" (with ice).*

1. Burn an orange peel over a cocktail glass.
2. If you want to serve the cocktail straight-up, shake all the ingredients in a cocktail shake and strain into a cocktail glass.
3. If you want to serve the cocktail on the rocks, add all the ingredients in a highball glass filled with ice and stir with a cocktail spoon.
4. If you find the drink too strong, add simple syrup to the mix.

## 4 MANHATTAN

2 oz whiskey
1 oz sweet vermouth
1 dash Angostura bitter
1 cherry

*The legend says that the drink was invented at the Manhattan Club by a bartender named Rob Roy when they were throwing a party for Winston Churchill's mother, Jennie. It has a very distinct flavor.*

1. Add all the ingredients into a mixing glass with ice.
2. Stir with a spoon and strain over a cocktail glass when chilled.
3. Garnish with a cherry.

# 5 CHAMPAGNE COCKTAIL

*Bubbly is the universal symbol for parties and one of the many reasons why Champagne is the perfect ingredient to use in "before dinner drinks" since they help stimulate your appetite. Feel free to substitute sparkling wine for Champagne.*

1 tsp Angostura bitter
1 sugar cube
Lemon peel for garnish
Champagne or sparkling
wine

1. Pour the Angostura bitter on top of the sugar cube and let it absorb.
2. Add the sugar cube to the bottom of a champagne glass.
3. Slowly pour the champagne over the sugar cube, holding the glass at a slight angle. The sugar cube will make extra bubbles, and gives the cocktail a flavor of cardamom. Garnish with a lemon peel.
4. If you want to show off you can always burn the lemon peel over the glass before composing the cocktail.

# 6 MARTINI

*Possibly the most famous drink of them all, the martini can be mixed using either vodka or gin as a base. No matter what James Bond says, a martini should always be stirred not shaken.*

3 oz of vodka or gin
¼ oz of vermouth (if you
    want a dry martini then
    use dry vermouth)
Olive
Olive brine (optional)

1. Add the ingredients to a mixing glass filled with ice.
2. Stir about fifty times if you are using large ice cubes, and about twenty-five times if you are using smaller cubes.
3. Strain the ice and pour into its signature glass. Garnish with an olive or two, preferably without the pimento in the middle. Can be served "dirty," with a splash of olive brine.

## Burnt Citrus Peel

By burning the peel of a lemon, orange, or lime over a cocktail glass, you add oils that are rich in citrus flavor. Here's how you do it: Wash the citrus fruit and cut out a dollar-coin-sized peel round. Avoid cutting too deep since you want to avoid the bitter white part of the peel, which is called the "pith." Hold the peel a few inches above the glass with the outer side of the peel facing into the glass. Light a match and hold it between the peel and the glass. Squeeze, allowing the oils to spurt into the glass. This technique is a great crowd pleaser that will enhance the flavor of any cocktail.

## Bubbly

Make your party a little bit more glamorous by serving individual portion-sized bottles of Champagne or sparkling wine. To make it more fun, skip the glasses and simply use straws. It looks so chic, it doesn't matter if you serve sparkling wine or its "fancier" cousin Champagne.

*1 Side Car  2 Tom Collins  3 Cosmopolitan  4 Manhattan  5 Champagne Cocktail  6 Martini*

## WHICH GLASS?

*Martini Glass*—is used for all "straight-up" cocktails, or drinks served without ice cubes in the glass.

*Highball Glass*—is for all mixed drinks served with ice cubes in the glass. Also used for soda and beer.

*Rocks Glass*—is for drinks served "on the rocks," or a single spirit poured over ice cubes with no mixer.

*Wine Glass*—is used for red and white wine and for frozen cocktails made with crushed ice.

*Port Glass*—is used to serve port, liqueur, or high-shelf spirits "straight up," without ice.

*Champagne Glass*—is for Champagne, sparkling wine, and Champagne cocktails.

## HOW MUCH DO I NEED?

Estimate two drinks per guest during the first hour of the party. For the following hours, estimate one drink per guest per hour.

– One bottle of Champagne (750 ml) yields approximately six glasses, but if you are performing a toast, fill the glasses only one-third of the way. In this case, one bottle will be enough for twelve guests.

– One bottle of alcohol (1 liter) yields approximately twenty-two drinks.

– One bottle of wine (750 ml) yields five glasses. Estimate one bottle for every three guests to be served during dinner. For the larger cocktail party, where more drinks will be consumed, one bottle for every eight guests will be plenty. Also note white wine is usually more popular than red.

### Tip!

Attach a unique ribbon around each glass's stem at your next cocktail party. This will allow your guests to recognize their glasses, even if they set them down for a minute while mingling. A nice touch and major dish saver!

### Mix It Up!

– Jell-O Shots. You've seen them in every bad college movie. However, this tacky shot can be spruced up. Make Jell-O just like your mom used to but instead of adding water to the mixture, use alcohol. For example, serve lime-flavored Jell-O with gin on a slice of lime and you have a creation that tastes surprisingly similar to gin & tonic.

– Drink Recipes. You don't have to be a bartender to come up with your own drinks. Name your creations so they relate to your party theme and remember to taste-test each one before your guests arrive. Not feeling creative? Simply find some old well-known recipes and rename them for the evening.

– Drinks for two. A hollowed-out coconut or a jumbo-sized milkshake glass is perfect for the 1-for-2 cocktail. Put two straws in each glass and let the guests share.

# GET THE PARTY STARTED

*O*n the pages that follow, you'll find recipes and tips that will help you throw fabulous parties of your own. Whether it's a cocktail party, brunch, buffet, or dinner party, use the information that follows as a guide for creating the perfect food, drink, and décor at your next party. As these are merely guidelines to help you along, don't be afraid to experiment and add your own personal touch to any event. Not only will this make them stand out to your guests, but it will also make them fun to plan.

# DRINKS, SNACKS & LATE-NIGHT BITES

EVERY GOOD PARTY *always starts with a drink. It will stand as the first impression your guests receive about the party, so you'll want to make it fun and memorable. This chapter is filled with fun drinks and snacks that work both at the begininning of a party, or as late-night snacks.*

## MENU

Boozy Pops
Snow Cone Bar
Flowering Punch Bowl

—

Parmesan-Truffle Popcorn
Spiced Nuts
Warm Chips & Truffled Dip

—

Homemade Condiments

—

Brewtini
Ice-Cubed Watermelon Spritzer
Americano Soda Pop

—

Grown-Ups' Milkshake
Boozy Donuts
Hot Toddy

# BOOZY POPS

A drink on a stick!

3 parts fresh peach juice
½ part lemon juice
½ part water
1 part fruit liqueur, such as Xante
    Pear Cognac

1. Combine all ingredients in a pitcher or cocktail shaker and pour into popsicle molds. Insert wooden stick and chill until frozen. Serve in a glass to avoid drips.

# SNOW CONE BAR

Forget the sugary snow cones of your childhood and try making fresh-fruit, adult snow cones at home. Super easy, delicious, and all you need is a blender.

1 cup of fresh fruit, cleaned
    and cut
½ cup of water
½ cup of sugar
1 cup fresh-squeezed lemon juice
½ cup liqueur
Ice

1. Fruit syrup. Add the fruit, sugar, and water in a saucepan, bring to a boil so the sugar melts. Add to your blender and mix until smooth, then set aside to cool.
2. Crush ice in blender to a fine "snow."
3. Ball the ice in a cone or cocktail glass, add 1 oz. of your homemade fruit syrup, and an equal part (1 oz.) lemon juice.

Some favorite adult flavor combinations:
Strawberry syrup & Xante Pear Liqueur
Raspberry syrup & Limoncello
Blood Orange syrup & Campari

> ### Tip!
>
> Set up a snow cone bar for your party and let your guests assemble their own cones; this works great as both a drink and a dessert.

# FLOWERING PUNCH BOWL

This beautiful punch with edible flowers acts as both a table decoration and a cocktail.

½ fresh pineapple
2 oranges, peeled and cut
1 sweet grapefruit, peeled and cut
½ cup pitted or frozen cherries
¼ cup of sugar
2 cups (16 oz.) Cherry Heering
    liqueur
2 bottles sparkling wine or
    Champagne

1. In a large bowl, muddle the fruit with sugar.
2. Pour the liqueur over the fruit and sugar, cover and let it sit for several hours in the refrigerator.
3. Stir the fruit and liquid and strain into the serving bowl.
4. Add the frozen flower ice cubes to the serving bowl right before guests arrive, and fill with sparkling wine or Champagne.

# FLOWER ICE CUBE

Edible flowers

1. Wash and clean a handful of edible flowers.
2. Fill a square Tupperware container half way with water, and add the flowers. Freeze for a couple of hours, fill up with water, and freeze until you have a large ice cube. Serve in the punch bowl.

# PARMESAN-TRUFFLE POPCORN

½ stick of salted butter
2 tbsp truffle oil
½ cup grated Parmesan cheese

This is one of my favorite go-to party snacks and it's the perfect finger food to serve in decorative paper bags that match your party's theme! It's easy to make and very inexpensive—though you couldn't tell by the flavor.

1. Melt the butter in a saucepan over low heat or in the microwave. Remove from heat and stir in truffle oil.
2. Drizzle mixture over popcorn, then add the Parmesan cheese.

# SPICED NUTS

2 tbsp olive oil
2 tbsp sugar
1 tsp sea salt
1 tbsp chopped rosemary
Dash of cayenne pepper
1 ½ cups almonds, such as
    Spanish Marcona almonds

1. Preheat your oven to 350°F.
2. In a saucepan, heat up olive oil, sugar, and cayenne pepper until the sugar melts and browns slightly. Add almonds, rosemary, and salt. Stir well.
3. Bake on a wax paper-lined baking sheet until golden.

# WARM CHIPS & TRUFFLED DIP

½ cup crème fraiche
2 tsp truffle or truffle paste
Sea salt and pepper to taste

I'm not the only person with a weakness for truffles, and chances are your guests feel the exact same way. This dip is a sure-fire party hit.

1. Mix the crème fraiche, truffle, and salt and pepper to taste.
2. While the dip sits, set your oven to 350°F and heat salted potato chips for 5 minutes.
3. Serve with hot dip.

# *HOMEMADE CONDIMENTS*

Making your own condiments is surprisingly easy and a great way to add a new touch to the good old cheese or smoked meat tray. Try the recipes below and make sure to tell your guests all about how you made these.

1 large red onion, peeled and
    roughly chopped
1 stick celery, trimmed and
    roughly chopped
Olive oil
2 cloves garlic, peeled and
    sliced
½ a fresh red chili, deseed and
    finely chopped
½ cup fresh parsley, leaves
    picked, stalks chopped
1 tbsp coriander seeds
1 tsp freshly ground black
    pepper
1 lb. cherry or plum tomatoes,
    halved
¾ cup + 2 tbsp red wine
    vinegar
⅓ cup brown sugar

### Homemade Ketchup

1. Place all the vegetables in a large heavy-bottomed saucepan with a big splash of olive oil and the garlic, chili, parsley stalks, coriander seeds, and cloves. Season with salt and pepper.
2. Cook gently over a low heat for 10 to 15 minutes until softened, stirring every so often. Add all the tomatoes and 1 ½ cups of cold water. Bring to the boil and simmer gently until the sauce reduces by half.
3. Add the sauce to food processor or blender, to make sure it's smooth. Put the sauce back in the pan and add the vinegar and sugar.
4. Place the sauce on medium heat and simmer until it reduces and thickens to the desired consistency. Taste and season additionally as needed.

2 peaches
1 red onion
2 garlic cloves
½ cup of sugar
1 cup fresh-squeezed lemon juice
½ cup liqueur
Ice

### Peach & Mustard Seed Chutney

This recipe also works with plums, and it's the perfect way to use up all those ripe peaches come September. Best of all, it will keep in the fridge for about two weeks. Simply pull out and serve.

1. In a large bowl, muddle the fruit with sugar.
2. Pour the liqueur over the fruit and sugar, cover and let it sit for several hours in the refrigerator.
3. Stir the fruit and liquid and strain into the serving bowl.
4. Add the frozen flower ice cubes to the serving bowl right before guests arrive, and fill with sparkling wine or Champagne.

3 cups heavy whipping cream
2 tbsp sea salt

### Homemade Butter

Everything tastes better when it's homemade—especially butter. This may just be the best butter you've ever tasted.

1. Add cream to a food processor and whip until thick, then will curdle and seperate into butter and buttermilk. Pour out the buttermilk out (or keep for pancakes) and keep whisking till fluffy and white, pouring off additional buttermilk as necessary.
2. Add salt and serve. Will keep in fridge for about a week.

1 Mexican beer, such as
    Corona or Sol
Juice of 1 lime
3 tbsp simple syrup
1.5 oz. tequila
½ oz. Cointreau or Triple sec

# BREWTINI

The brewtini, and other beer-based cocktails like the Michelada, have been for some time, but they are back with a vengeance behind the bars.

1. In a blender, combine the tequila, lime juice, simply syrup and cointreau with 5 ice cubes. Blend into a slushy mix.
2. In a large glass, combine the beer and slushy mix and serve up.

½ cups of cubed watermelon
1 skewer
½ lemon wedge
2 oz. vodka
Sparkling water

# ICE-CUBED WATERMELON SPRITZER

This is such an easy drink to make and the watermelon ice cubes add a fun and functional touch. Also works well as a non-alcoholic "mocktail." Simply hold the vodka.

1. Put the watermelon cubes on the skewer and freeze.
2. When ready to serve, build cocktail in a highball glass, by adding lemon juice, vodka, and iced watermelon skewer, top with chilled sparkling water and serve.

1 oz. Campari
1 oz. sweet vermouth
Club soda
1 orange wheel

# AMERICANO SODA POP

This is actually based on a classic Italian cocktail called "The Americano," known for its popularity amongst expats. I like to serve it up like an adult soda pop.

1. Fill a glass with ice, add the Campari, and sweet vermouth and club soda; stir well.
2. Garnish with an orange wheel.

1 cup milk
1 scoop vanilla ice cream
1 shot espresso
1 ½ oz. coffee liqueur
1 pinch of salt

# GROWN-UPS' MILKSHAKE

1. Combine all ingredients in a blender, blend, and serve up.

# BOOZY DONUTS WITH CRÈME BRÛLÉE TOPPING

Donuts are the new cupcakes, and this is an easy way to spruce-up a plain, store-bought donut from afternoon snack to fun dessert.

6 sugar-covered donuts
½ cup of sugar
3 oz. liqueur of choice

1. Heat the donuts in the oven at 250 degrees for 5 minutes.
2. Pour the sugar on a plate, brush the top of the warm donuts with water and dip in the sugar.
3. Insert and fill the liqueur in multiple spots in the bottom of the donuts with a small turkey baster/or cake decorating tool.
4. Using a brûlée torch, burn the sugar on top of the donuts until it becomes a hard sugar topping.

1 cup Xante Pear Cognac
5 cups of fresh apple juice or cider
5 cinnamon sticks
3 cardamom pods
2 whole cloves
1 tbsp unsalted butter
½ lemon, cut into wheels
A dash of apple cider vinegar

# HOT TODDY

Warm guests up when they arrive on those cool autumn evenings with this cozy cocktail. It's also the perfect way to send off guests before they head out into the cold.

1. Add the apple cider to a pot along with the spices.
2. Heat on low for 20 minutes, remove from heat and add the butter and lemon wheels.
3. Pour in cognac and sift off the spices before serving hot.

# COCKTAIL PARTY

*Starts between 5 PM and 8 PM*
*The classic "mingling" party.*

## MENU

Raspberry and Rose Martinis

Ginger Flavored Elderberry Martinis

Chocolate Truffle Martinis

French Fries with 3 Dips

Scandinavian Ceviche

Modern Cheese Tray

Mini Hamburgers with Foie Gras

Rosemary Skewers with Prosciutto and
Monk Fish

Smoked Salmon Chips

Grapefruit and Campari Sorbet with
Mini Marshmallows

Truffled Mini Cupcakes

COCKTAIL PARTIES BECAME *trendy in the 1920s during Prohibition times. The economy was booming, and New York socialites would try to trump each other by throwing parties, each more lavish than the next. With Prohibition in full swing, these events were hosted in private homes where hosts and guests alike could sneak the occasional drink every now and then. It was also during prohibition times that women started to play a greater role in the social scene, which ultimately lead to it becoming acceptable for women to drink in the company of men.*

## DÉCOR

Sticking to your party theme is easy when organizing a cocktail party. —matching invitations and decorative trays are all you really need. If you want to go all out, you can decorate the space as well. Just remember to place all your decorations at eye level since guests will be standing throughout the event. One large flower arrangement in the middle of the room is always a safe bet. A true cocktail party is always a bit crammed, so hold the gathering in one room— it encourages mingling.

## FOOD

The food served at a cocktail party is collectively called "hors d'oeuvres," which is essentially defined as small finger food that your guests should be able to eat without a plate, in only a bite or two. Since the quantities of food are small, go for quality ingredients.

Hors d'oeuvres are divided into three categories: hot hors d'oeuvres, cold hors d'oeuvres, and canapés. What makes a canapé a canapé, and not a hors d'oeuvre, is that it has a flat and edible base, much like an open-faced sandwich; small squares of bread, crackers, or potato chips are all great bases for canapés. Traditionally, snacks from all three categories are served and the larger the party, the greater the variety of hors d'oeuvres there should be. Be creative when you plan your menu; any dish can be turned into a canapé or hors d'oeuvre. Your famous stew can be served in small hollowed-out puff pastry balls or your favorite chocolate cake can be cut into small pieces and served on a skewer with a strawberry. As always, don't forget to have at least one vegetarian alternative. Always serve more hearty alternatives at the beginning of the party, and finish with lighter treats like dessert hors d'oeuvres.

# SERVICE

Serve the hors d' oeuvres neatly, preferably in rows on trays. Make it more festive by using unexpected objects, such as laminated records, Plexiglass or picture frames, as serving trays. Bowls holding dipping sauces or candles should be attached to the tray with double-sided tape or by placing a lemon slice underneath to avoid slips. Between servings, seltzer water is the easiest, and most food-friendly, way to freshen up sticky trays.

Cocktail service traditionally involves the host or hostess walking the room with serving trays . In the home, service can be simplified by placing one cold hors d'oeuvres on a table so that guests can help themselves while you are working in the kitchen or circling the room. In the absence of plates, you will need plenty of napkins so hold the serving tray with one hand and a bundle of serviettes in the other one. Put a plate, stocked with napkins, next to the cold hors d'oeuvres table and tie a ribbon around them to make sure they stay put. Smaller cocktail napkins, no bigger than 6 x 6 inches, should be used and always make sure you have four times as many as the amount of guests, plus more at the bar.

Try to find serviettes that match your theme or personalize plain napkins by using stamps with a simple motif or your initials. Make sure there are drop tables where guests can put their used glasses and napkins.

# DRINKS

Simplify by premixing drinks in pitchers well in advance or serving them in a punch bowl; just waitto add the ice until right before your guests arrive—no one likes a watery cocktail! All you need to do when the first guest arrives is stir, strain into garnished glasses, and serve on trays.

All cocktails in this chapter can be easily prepared in advance. Generally, two different types of cocktails for the evening should suffice (for example, one with a gin base and another with vodka). By premixing, you save both time and cash since you decide the strength of the cocktails ahead of time, and you won't have to stock up on supplies for a full bar. The advantages of a bar, however, are that guests can request their favorite drinks, and it can be a popular spot to gather, talk, and make new acquaintances. Either set up a DIY bar or ask a friend to play bartender for the evening.

Make sure you always have water and a nonalcoholic alternative available at any cocktail party. Beer is not generally served, but wine and/ or Champagne is perfectly acceptable. Individual mini-Champagne bottles served with a straw are a great bar-free alternative. Serve sweet dessert cocktails to signal the party has come to an end.

## Tip!

State on the invitation when the party starts. If you'd like to avoid lingering guests, you can also add an ending time. A traditional cocktail party has at least twelve guests.

## Hors d'oeuvre Facts

Tradition states that the more guests you invite, the more food options you should serve.

| Guests | Hors d'oeuvres |
|--------|----------------|
| 12–16 | 3–4 types minimum |
| 17–25 | 4–5 types minimum |
| 26+ | 5–6 types minimum |

## How Much Do People Eat?

Figure two of each type of hors d'oeuvres per guest if the party lasts a couple of hours. Take these other factors into consideration:

* Timing. After work, guests will be hungry and eat more, so figure three of each type instead of two. If the party is held later in the evening, guests will already have eaten and the food will last longer.

* Cocktail hour. Are you planning on serving hors d'oeuvres followed by dinner? Figure about one of each type instead of two.

* Guests. Elderly people and women tend to eat less, so consider your crowd when estimating how much food to serve.

# RASPBERRY AND ROSE MARTINI

3 oz. vodka
2 oz. raspberry
   puree
1 oz. raspberry
   liquor
Edible, non-toxic
   rose leaves

1. Wash the rose leaves thoroughly and mix with the vodka. Let the mixture sit overnight, or until you are ready to serve your drinks. Strain the flavored vodka.
2. Combine the puree and vodka in a cocktail shaker with ice and strain the drink into a martini glass.
3. Top the drink with raspberry liquor and decorate with a thoroughly cleaned rose leaf.

**Tip!**
Easily make your own raspberry puree by boiling equal parts sugar and water to make simple syrup. Puree raspberries in a blender, then add the simple syrup to taste. It's quick, easy, and adds a huge boost of flavor!

# GINGER ELDERBERRY MARTINI

½ oz. simple syrup
1 pinch dried and
   ground ginger
1 oz. concentrated
   elderberry syrup
1 oz. lime juice
3 oz. gin
Lime wedge

1. Boil simple syrup, then add the dried ground ginger. Let the syrup cool to room temperature.
2. Add all the ingredients to a cocktail shaker with ice. Shake and strain into a martini glass.
3. Garnish with a lime wedge.

**Tip!**
In a hurry? Substitute ginger ale for simple syrup and ginger. If you want to add an extra twist, decorate the rim of the glass with a mixture of sugar and dried, ground ginger. Mix sugar and the ginger on a plate then dampen the rim of the glass by using a lime wedge. Dip the glass in the sugar mixture. You can also simply decorate by adding a piece of crystallized or candied ginger.

Elderberry syrup can be found in gourmet grocery stores.

**Tip!**

All drink recipes yield one drink at a time using a cocktail shaker. If you are making cocktails for a crowd, multiply and mix the ingredients in a pitcher. When the guests arrive simply add ice, stir, and strain into martini glasses. This might not be proper bar etiquette, but it's definitely a time saver.

# CHOCOLATE TRUFFLE MARTINI

2 oz. orange/mandarin
   vodka
3 oz. chocolate liquor
1 chocolate truffle
Orange peel

1. Burn orange peel over a martini glass.
2. Mix the vodka and liquor with ice in a separate mixing glass. Stir well.
3. Place a chocolate truffle in the bottom of the cocktail glass with the citrus oil. Strain the beverage into the cocktail glass.

**Tip!**
If you are serving a larger quantity of chocolate truffle martinis at the same time, it can be a chore to burn orange peel into each one. Instead, cut an orange peel into a spiral shape and serve, as a garnish, in each glass. By cutting it in a spiral, more flavor will seep into the drink. You can also serve the drink with a rim of half unsweetened cocoa powder and half sugar. Swirl an orange wedge along the rim, and then dip the glass rim in the mixture.

Chocolate truffles can be bought in gourmet grocery and specialty stores.

# *FRENCH FRIES WITH THREE DIPS*

**Serves 4 guests**

4 large potatoes
1 tsp vegetable oil
Salt

1. Turn your oven to 425°F.
2. Peel the potatoes and cut them into equal sized sticks, about a ½-inch wide. Toss the pieces that are too small, as they will burn in the oven.
3. Rinse the potatoes pieces and place them in a large pot of boiling salted water. Boil for 2 minutes. Strain the potatoes and rinse them in cold water, leaving until cool. Place the potato sticks on a layer of paper towels and to dry.
4. Once dried, place the potatoes on a baking sheet lined with parchment paper. Drizzle with oil and toss the potatoes by hand until well coated. Spread the potatoes evenly on the baking sheet, and make sure that the potato pieces are not touching each other.
5. Bake the potatoes in the middle rack of your oven for about 30 minutes. Turn the potatoes after about 15 minutes so they get even color.

### Rosemary Mayonnaise

½ cup mayonnaise
2 tsp fresh chopped rosemary
Salt and pepper to taste

1. Mix the mayo and rosemary.
2. Let it sit for at least an hour in the fridge. When you are ready to serve the sauce, add salt and pepper to taste.

### Wasabi Mustard

2 tbsp of Dijon mustard
4 tbsp of crème fraiche
½ tsp of wasabi
Salt and white pepper to taste

1. Mix the mustard and crème fraiche in a bowl and add the wasabi. Start with ¼ tsp and taste the mixture. Add the rest until you achieve the desired spiciness. Keep in mind that the flavor will be enhanced the longer the dipping sauce sits.
2. Let the mixture sit for at least an hour in the fridge. When you are ready to serve the sauce, add salt and pepper to taste.

### Curry Ketchup

2 cup ketchup
2 tsp curry

1. Mix the ketchup and curry, and let it sit for at least an hour in the fridge.

*Serving tip:*
Nothing says "party" like individual serving cups—they are easy for your guests to hold while mingling, not to mention they look great. Serve the fries in cones made out of any decorative paper or even something as simple as newspaper. Roll the paper into proportionate cones, line them with wax paper, and staple them at the edge. Serve the cones on a tray with the dipping sauces. Make the perfect tray by punching holes in a box lid and placing one cone in each hole.

*Simplify:*
Buy frozen French fries from your grocery store that just need to be heated or even ready-made ones from a restaurant. Get rid of the "evidence" and serve in decorative cones with your homemade sauces—your guests will never know!

*For a challenge:*
Chop fresh herbs and mix with the hot pommes frites (French for "French fries") when they come out of the oven. It only takes a second and it looks, smells, and tastes great. You can also use different colored potatoes, such as red skinned, orange sweet potatoes, or blue potatoes of the delta blue variety.

# SCANDINAVIAN CEVICHE

**Serves 4 guests**

1 grapefruit
½ avocado
4 oz. pre-sliced gravlax, or
  smoked salmon
2 tbsp finely diced red onion

1. Filet the grapefruit by first cutting off the peel so that the citrus flesh is exposed. Then cut out the filets by angling the knife and cutting by the natural partings. The filets come out in half moon shapes. Cut the into ½-inch pieces.
2. Peel and finely dice the red onion. Peel the avocado and cut into ½-inch cubes. Do the same with the salmon slices.
3. Mix all the ingredients in a plastic bowl or plastic bag. Let the mixture soak for at least an hour in the fridge before serving.

*Serving tip!*
Serve the ceviche in shot glasses with a teaspoon. It tastes best cool, so serve the shot glasses on a deep tray filled with ice.

*Simplify:*
This dish keeps well in the refrigerator and can be prepared up to twenty-four hours beforehand; the citrus juice ensures the avocado doesn't turn brown.

*For a challenge:*
Make a more traditional ceviche by using raw fish, shrimp, or scallops. Use lime juice instead of grapefruit, and add chopped tomatoes and cilantro. Use a white fish, such as cod or snapper. Always freeze the fish for at least 3 days before you use it to kill any possible parasites.

# MODERN CHEESE TRAY

3 oz. assorted cheeses per person

Serving a cheese tray may sound horribly dated but it's still one of the most popular offerings at any event and the flavor variations are virtually endless, so it can be tailored for any situation. Cheese is usually produced from goat's, sheep's, water buffalo's, or cow's milk using many different techniques. Just because one type of cheese is produced using one specific technique doesn't mean it will taste the same time and time again. On the contrary, they will often taste completely different depending on where in the world the cheese is produced. Choose various types of cheese with different firmnesses and from different countries to achieve a good spread. Don't forget artisanal cheeses from America are world class.

### Serving tip!
Serve the cheese at room temperature to enhance the flavor, together with bread, fruit, and homemade marmalades and compotes. Place the cheese tray on a table and leave it there throughout the party so your guests always have access.

### Simplify:
Ask for help at your grocery store's cheese counter if you're unsure about what varieties to pick as they are more than willing to help you choose an interesting mix. If you don't make your own preserves, buy ready-made marmalades or jams.

### For a Challenge:
Homemade bread is a perfect complement to any cheese (try the recipe on p139).

Serves 4 guests

### Apricot and Chili Marmalade

6 oz. good quality apricot marmalade
2 tsp chili flakes

1. Heat up the marmalade and chili flakes over low heat. Make sure it doesn't boil. Taste it; the mixture should have a light, hot aftertaste.
2. Serve warm.

### Truffle Honey

6 oz. honey
3 tbsp of truffle oil
Salt and pepper to taste

1. Lightly heat up the honey so that it melts. Add the truffle oil, and salt and pepper to taste.
2. Let it cool down and serve at room temperature.

### Port Wine Poached Dates

¼ cup port wine
½ cup dates
Pepper to taste

1. Give the dates a rough chop. Add to a saucepan with the port wine. Bring to a simmer over low heat for 15 minutes, or until the sauce has thickened.
2. Season with pepper to taste.

# CHEESE TERMINOLOGY

*Fromage*—the French word for cheese
*Cendre*—the French name for cheese that has been ripened in ash
*Pecorino*—the Italian name for cheese made with sheep's milk
*Ferme/Fermier*—the French name for cheese produced on a farm
*Coulant*—the French name for runny cheeses such as a Brie or Camembert
*Capra*—the Italian name for goat's-milk cheese
*Chèvre*—the French word for goat, used to describe all goat's-milk cheeses
*Bleu*—the French word for blue, used to describe blue cheese/blue-vein cheese
*Tome*—the French word used to describe cheeses produced in the mountain regions

## QUICK GUIDE TO IMPORTED CHEESES

### FRESH OR UNRIPENED CHEESE
*Feta*—Greek sheep's or goat's-milk cheese, salted
*Mascarpone*—cheese from Italy, made with cow's milk and commonly used for desserts since it has a sweet flavor
*Mozzarella*—cheese from Italy, traditionally made with water buffalo milk, also has a sweet flavor
*Ricotta*—cheese from Italy, consistency similar to cottage cheese, traditionally used in pasta sauces

### SOFT CHEESE
*Cheeses with a thin skin and a creamy center*
*Brie*—French rind-ripened cheese made from cow's milk
*Camembert*—French rind-ripened cheese, made with cow's milk similar to Brie but with a slightly milder flavor
*Boursin*—French triple cream cow's-milk cheese, usually flavored with spices and herbs

### SEMI-SOFT CHEESE
*Cheese with a soft and sliceable texture*
*Fontina*—Italian cow's milk cheese
*Gorgonzola*—the famous blue vein Italian cow's-milk cheese, which is much creamier than Stilton or Roquefort
*Havarti*—Danish cow's-milk cheese, often flavored with dill
*Gouda*—Dutch cheese with a red or yellow wax, made from cow's milk and has a creamy texture
*Roquefort*—French blue-vein cheese, made with sheep's milk
*Stilton*—British blue-vein cheese made from cow's milk.

### FIRM CHEESE
*Cheddar*—the world's most famous cheese is a cow's-milk cheese produced both in Great Britain and the United States. It is naturally white, but is sometimes dyed orange. Tastes best when made from raw milk and aged.
*Emmentaler*—Swiss cow's-milk cheese
*Gruyère*—Swiss cow's-milk cheese that is similar in taste to emmentaler, but is aged longer and has a stronger flavor.
*Provolone*—flavorful Italian cheese, made from cow's milk. Dolce is aged for 2 months, Piccante for 6 months. It also comes smoked.

### HARD CHEESE
*Cheeses that are aged and usually very flavorful*
*Asiago*—Italian flavorful cow's-milk cheese that is aged for at least 2 years
*Parmigiano-Reggiano (Parmesan)*—Italian cow's-milk cheese, made exclusively in the region near Parma. One of the world's oldest and most copied cheeses.
*Percorino-Romano*—Italian sheep's-milk cheese from southern Italy.

## Cheesy Trends
These days cheese has become a hot topic among foodies. Chefs are going on cheese trips instead of wine tastings, and people are leaving their 9 to 5 jobs to become "apprentices" at tiny cheese farms in the country. Why not arrange your own cheese tasting? Invite your friends over and ask them to bring one cheese and learn a little about it for the evening. Everyone can share what they've learned during the tasting.

## Tip!
– Spanish cheeses are usually of the finest quality and taste, but are overshadowed by their famous French competition. You can usually get a great-tasting Spanish cheese for a lot less money than a French one, so keep that in mind.

– Cheese can be paired with anything from amber beer to hard apple cider, but most people still prefer pairing with wine. As a rule of thumb: choose cheeses and wines from the same region.

# MINI HAMBURGERS WITH FOIE GRAS

**Serves 4 guests**

4 oz. of good-quality ground
    beef (max 10 percent fat content)
4 mini-hamburger buns
4 tsp mayonnaise
4 thin slices (1 oz.) of foie gras
Salt and pepper

1. Set your oven to broil. Split the ground beef into 4 equal parts and shape them into mini-burger patties. Salt and pepper them well on both sides.
2. Place the patties on a baking sheet lined with parchment paper and broil them high up in the oven for approximately 6 minutes, 3 minutes on each side.
3. Split the mini-hamburger buns, and place them in the oven the last minute so that they become warm and slightly toasted.
4. Add mayonnaise and pepper on the inside of the buns, place the beef patty on the bottom half of the bun, then add the slice of foie gras. This way it will melt slightly. Top with the other half of the bun and spear with a toothpick to keep everything in place.

*Simplify:*
If you are having a hard time finding mini-hamburger buns, use mini-potato rolls, brioche bread, or simply split a regular-sized bun in half. You can also substitute foie gras for duck or goose liver pate.

*For a challenge:*
Instead of a regular toothpick, use a Japanese skewer with a little stylish knot on top. Add a little cognac and a touch of cayenne to the mayonnaise to add another dimension of flavor. For the best flavor boost, buy sirloin and grind it in your food processor for about fifteen seconds to make your own beef patties.

*Foie Gras* may not be politically correct, but it is definitely delicious. Made from goose or duck liver from birds that have been force fed to get an extra fatty liver, its production has become quite controversial. Foie gras isn't commonly used in American cooking, but it's a classic hors d'oeuvre ingredient. It comes in metal cans similar to spam and stores almost as long, so if you happen to be passing through France, pick some up—it's worth every penny.

# ROSEMARY SKEWERS WITH PROSCIUTTO AND MONK FISH

**Serves 4 guests**

12 oz. monkfish, cod or other
    firm, white fish
4 rosemary sprigs
4 slices of prosciutto ham
Salt and pepper

1. Cut the fish in 1 inch square pieces. Salt and pepper them lightly.
2. Rinse the rosemary sprigs and cut them to about 5 inch long skewers. Clean off the leaves, leaving only a few at the top for presentation.
3. Skewer the fish pieces with the rosemary sprigs, and wrap the ham around the fish.
4. Grill the skewer in the oven with your broiler at 425°F for 4 minutes per side. Serve hot out of the oven.

**Citrus creme**

½ tbsp grated lemon zest
2 tbsp lemon juice
2 tbsp coarsely chopped shallots
1 tsp unsalted butter
5 tbs crème fraiche (or sour
    cream)
Salt and white pepper

1. Wash the lemons well in warm water and zest the peel on a grater, without getting any of the bitter, white pith. Juice the lemon and reserve. Peel and coarsely chop the shallots.
2. Melt the butter in a small saucepan. Once the butter is hot and stops bubbling, add the shallots and sauté them until they become translucent. Add the lemon zest, followed by the juice.
3. Take the pan off the heat, and stir in the crème fraiche. Salt and pepper to taste.
4. Pour the sauce into 4 small shot glasses or decorative cups, and serve the skewers on top.

*Serving tip!*
By serving the skewers on top of, or in, the sauce cup, your guests can walk around and mingle while eating without having to worry about drips and the dreaded double-dip.

*Simplify:*
Rosemary skewers can be prepared up to twenty-four hours in advance, and will taste even better after resting to allow the rosemary flavor to permeate the raw fish. Just pop them in the oven when the guests arrive.

*For a challenge:*
Fish will absorb the flavor of the rosemary, so the herb works both as a seasoning and skewer. Test out other herb skewers, such as thyme or sage. For a different flavor in the sauce, try using Moroccan preserved lemon peel instead of fresh lemon. It adds an exotic salty/sour flavor.

# SMOKED SALMON CHIPS

**Serves 4 guests**

6 slices of smoked salmon
12 large potato chips
2 tbsp crème fraiche (or sour cream)
Chive, thyme or dill for decoration

1. Divide each salmon slice in two, roll them to an appropriate size, and place them on the chips.
2. Put the crème fraiche in a plastic bag and cut a little hole in one corner to make the bag work as a piping bag. Pipe about ½ tsp onto each salmon chip.
3. Decorate with chive, thyme, or dill.

*Simplify:*
Take it easy on yourself by placing all the ingredients on a tray and letting your guests compose their own hors d'oeuvres.

*For a challenge:*
Spice it up by using different types of chips such as sweet potato, delta blue potato, or daikon radish. This recipe works well with caviar instead of salmon, too. If you're feeling really adventurous, you can even make your own chips in the oven with thin slices of potatoes.

# GRAPEFRUIT AND CAMPARI SORBET WITH MINI MARSHMALLOWS

**Serves 4 guests**

2 limes
4 scoops of grapefruit sorbet
4 tbsp Campari
⅛ cup mini marshmallows

1. Cut a thin sliver of peel at both ends of the limes. This will create a smooth bottom so they can stand securely. Split the lime in half, and remove all the flesh with a teaspoon or melon scooper. Place the emptied lime halves in the freezer for at least an hour.
2. Use a melon baller or tablespoon to scoop the sorbet into a size that will fit in the lime halves. Place a scoop in each lime and place in the freezer until serving time.
3. When ready to serve, pour a tablespoon of Campari over each scoop, and garnish with mini marshmallows. Serve with a teaspoon and cocktail napkin.

*Simplify:*
Campari is a bitter tasting aperitif from Italy that has a strong red color, and is usually served with soda. It might not be something you have at home, but it's worth a try. You can also try other combinations such as orange sorbet with port wine, or lemon sorbet with Limoncello or ice wine.

*For a challenge:*
If you happen to have an ice-cream maker at home, break it out of storage and try making your own sorbet. It's a lot easier and quicker than making ice cream from scratch and it tastes great.

# TRUFFLED MINI CUPCAKES

**Makes 20 mini cupcakes**

3½ oz. of butter
7 oz. of good-quality dark
   chocolate, recommended
   60% or above
   cacao content
2 eggs
½ cup sugar
1 tsp salt
½ tsp baking powder
½ cup flour
3 tsp cacao powder

4 oz of good quality
   chocolate
¼ cup heavy cream
Edible roses for
   decoration

1. Preheat your oven to 350°F. Melt the butter and the chocolate in a microwave oven at a low temperature in short bursts. Stir every thirty seconds until completely melted and lump free.
2. Beat the eggs with the sugar until white in color and fluffy. Mix the salt, baking powder, cacao powder, and flour in a separate small bowl.
3. Slowly and carefully add a little of the melted chocolate mix, and then a little of the flour mix into the egg mixture, alternating melted chocolate and flour until it's all mixed in. Do not over mix.
4. Fill small muffin cups ⅓ full of the batter. Bake in the middle of the oven for 15–17 minutes. When done, the cupcakes should still be sticky in the middle.
5. Take out of the oven and let them cool on a baking rack.

### Ganache – Chocolate Truffle Icing

1. Using a knife or your food processor, cut the chocolate into tiny pieces—the smaller the better.
2. Heat the cream on the stove until it boils. Keep a watchful eye on it since it will easily boil over. Pour the boiling cream slowly over the chocolate flakes, and stir until the chocolate is completely melted.
3. Allow to cool slightly, then use to decorate the top of the cooled cupcakes. Let it stiffen before serving.

Ganache is typically used to dip chocolate truffles in and create a finishing layer.

### Serving tip!
Believe it or not, salt is a great flavor enhancer for chocolate. Try putting a few flakes of sea salt on top of the cupcakes before serving them. Decorate with well-cleaned, edible roses or other edible flowers to spruce up this mini-dessert.

### Simplify:
Make the cupcakes up to a week in advance and freeze them. Make the ganache frosting and decorate on the day of the party.

### For a challenge:
Mix sugar with well-cleaned, edible rose petals, and let it sit for at least two days. Use the sugar when baking to add a rose flavor to the cupcakes, or anything else that you might be baking.

# BRUNCH

*Starts between 11 AM and 1 PM*
*Casual, easy, and a time saver.*

## MENU

Wasabi Bloody Mary

Valencia Mimosa

—

Banana Bread with Honey Butter

Chive Waffles with Horseradish Cream

Salmon en Papillote with Orange and Fresh Herb Sauce

Spinach and Asparagus Salad With
Poached Eggs

—

Yogurt Rice Pudding with Grilled Fruit
Skewers

BRUNCH IS, *as the name implies, a combination of breakfast and lunch. And while brunch is now a weekly occurrence for some, it wasn't until the end of the 19th century that the British upper class started hosting their own hunting parties where servants would arrange extravagant picnics, some of which included over-the-top decorations such as chandeliers hung from trees.*

*It wasn't until the 1930s that Hollywood put modern-day brunch on the map. During that time, movie stars frequently traveled by train to Los Angeles and New York City between movie productions. This transcontinental trip made a stop in Chicago, and celebrities used this opportunity to enjoy big, lunch-like breakfasts at the then world-famous Ambassador Hotel. After that, everybody wanted to "do brunch."*

## DÉCOR

Decorate your brunch according to your theme, but think in terms of quality, not quantity. Bring out your best china, and skip the stapling, taping, and cheating you can get away with at an evening party, as daylight will expose any flaws. Brunch works well the morning after you've hosted a large event with out-of-towners, like a bridal shower, bachelor/bachelorette party, or engagement party. While eating, you get a chance to chat and gossip about the previous night, and it makes travelers feel extra appreciated. Brunch can also kick-off a day together with friends. Catch up while enjoying your homemade creations, and then hit that shopping spree, pilates class, or planned museum visit. Match the theme with the planned activity.

### Tip!

Crazy schedule? Brunch is the perfect party. Quick, easy, and over by 2 PM. After saying good-bye to your guests, you still have plenty of time to run all your errands, plan other activities or just relax. You deserve it!

## FOOD

Your guests will arrive hungry since it is the first meal of the day, so be prepared to sit down as soon as everyone has arrived and whatever you do, don't be stingy with the food. As the name suggests, the food being served should be a fusion between breakfast and lunch, with the emphasis on lunch. If your guests had a late night the evening before, keep that in mind when planning your menu since they probably will be craving a heavier meal. Considering brunch's Anglo-Saxon origin, most traditional brunches offer sausages, bacon, pancakes, and scrambled eggs but there are no rules. Serve what you think fits your theme and what you think your guests will enjoy. At a spa-brunch, for instance, you might toast your own muesli and serve together with lychee and lime yogurt, multi-grain toast, and fresh-squeezed juice. Unless you are an early bird, prepare as much of your menu as possible the night before to cut down on the prep the day of.

## SERVICE

Brunch is a relaxed affair commonly hosted during the weekend when guests' schedules allow. You can choose either to serve it as a buffet or seated meal. If you are serving it seated, then set your table after traditional dinner guidelines (see "table setting," p.50–63). Buffet style is the most common way to serve brunch. (See "Buffet," p. 131-150 for set up details.) If you have a large dining table, you can conveniently combine the two serving styles. Set half the table dinner style, and use the other half to set up your buffet. This way you can seat and serve your guests at the same table. Use two tablecloths to differentiate the different sides of the table. Traditionally, brunch is a small, seated, and intimate affair served at a single table, but it will work for most event sizes. Host a brunch birthday bash, or even a brunch the day after a wedding for out-of-towners and close family. As always, don't forget to have seating for everyone.

## DRINKS

The truth about any party is that guests will come for the food, but they'll stay for the drinks and nothing makes a good brunch like bottomless Bloody Marys and mimosas. The Mimosa, a combination of orange juice and Champagne or sparkling wine, is said to have been first mixed in the Ritz Hotel, Paris, 1952. Bloody Marys, on the other hand, came to be just after World War I when the French began importing tomato juice from America. The drink was originally mixed using gin, but in the 1960s, Smirnoff started using the drink in their marketing campaigns, and it remains a mostly vodka-based drink to this day. Complement your brunch cocktail selection with tea, coffee, and fresh juices.

# WASABI BLOODY MARY

1 oz. vodka
2 dashes of Worcestershire sauce
2 dashes of Tabasco or other hot sauce
¼ oz. lemon juice
Pinch of wasabi, preferably paste
4 oz. tomato juice
Salt and pepper
Lemon slice
Cocktail tomato for garnish

1. Mix the sauces, wasabi, and juice. Stir well and flavor with salt and pepper to taste.
2. Fill the serving glass halfway with ice, and add the vodka and juice mixture. Stir well.
3. Decorate with a lemon slice and cocktail tomato on a skewer.

*Tip!*
Prepare the juice mixture well in advance—the mix will taste more flavorful after having time to sit and it makes your brunch easier to prepare in the morning.

# VALENCIA MIMOSA

2 oz. fresh orange juice
1 oz. apricot liquor
4 oz. Champagne or sparkling wine

1. First pour the orange juice into a Champagne glass or flute then add Champagne. To avoid losing precious bubbles, don't stir, but pull the juice up along the sides with a spoon.
2. Top with the apricot liquor.

# *BANANA BREAD*
# *WITH*
# *HONEY BUTTER*

**Serves 4 guests**

3 well-ripened bananas
3 oz. butter
½ cup sugar
2 eggs
1½ cup flour
½ cup muesli
½ tsp salt
1 tsp vanilla extract
2 tsp baking powder
3 tbsp brown sugar


4 oz. butter
4 tbsp honey
1 tsp coarse sea salt

1. Preheat your oven to 350°F. Peel the bananas and use a fork to crush two of them. Slice the third one.
2. Melt the butter. Meanwhile, beat the sugar and eggs until fluffy and white. Once the butter has cooled, slowly add it to the egg mixture.
3. Mix the flour, baking powder, and salt in a separate bowl. Slowly add the flour mix to the egg mix, and then do the same with the crushed bananas.
4. Butter and flour a cake pan, approximately 5 x 8 inch. Pour the batter into the pan, and top it with the last sliced banana and brown sugar.
5. Bake in the middle of the oven for 25–30 minutes. Check the bread with a toothpick. If it is dry, the bread is ready.


**Honey Butter**

1. Leave the butter out, allowing it to reach room temperature. This takes about an hour.
2. Stir the butter and drizzle the honey, mixing it slightly so it creates a layered effect. Add the salt on top.

*Simplify:*
You can mix the batter the day before, and store it in the baking pan ready to pop in the oven. It's important to keep the batter cool as you are preparing it, and store it in the refrigerator so the baking powder does not begin to rise before it goes into the oven.

*For a challenge:*
To make healthier bread, you can experiment with different types of flour. You can also add less flour and more muesli and walnuts for a heartier loaf.

# *CHIVE WAFFLES WITH HORSERADISH CREAM*

**Serves 4 guests**

5 oz. butter
1 cup flour
½ cup whole wheat flour
2 tsp baking powder
1 tsp salt
5 tbsp chopped chives
1 cup milk
1 cup water

½ cup of heavy whipping cream
2 tbsp of grated horse radish
salt and white pepper

1. Melt the butter in a saucepan while you heat the waffle iron.
2. Mix all the dry ingredients and add the chopped chives. Add the milk, water, and finally the melted butter. The consistency should be thick.
3. Brush the waffle iron with a little melted butter before you add the batter. Add an appropriate amount of batter depending on the size of your iron. Let the waffle cook until golden and crispy.

**Horseradish Cream**

1. Whip the cream until stiff peaks are created, and then add the horseradish. Salt and pepper to taste.

*Simplify:*
When serving multiple guests it can be time consuming to bake the waffles and keep them warm until they are ready to serve. As an alternative, create a waffle station where the guests can make their own. It's fun and social for the guests, and you can relax and enjoy a mimosa instead of being held hostage in the kitchen.

*For a challenge:*
This savory waffle recipe can replace toast on your brunch menu and goes well with salmon. You can also experiment with different waffle batters and let your guests pick their favorites. Make a sweet waffle batter by adding vanilla, or try one with spinach and lemon peel.

# SALMON EN PAPILLOTE WITH ORANGE AND FRESH HERB SAUCE

Serves 4 guests

1 pound of salmon fillet
Parchment paper
3 oz. of unsalted butter
2 tbsp lemon zest
2 oz. leaks
3 oz. fennel
2 oz. carrots
2 oz. celery
1 egg
Salt and pepper to taste

1. Turn your oven to 425°F. Split the salmon into four equal-size portions. Cut the parchment paper into four heart shapes. The hearts should be large enough to wrap the salmon pieces.
2. Melt ¼ of the butter. Mix the remaining butter with salt, pepper, and lemon zest to taste.
3. Wash and peel the vegetables. Cut them into matchsticks, also called julienne style.
4. Brush one side of the heart shapes with the melted butter, and place the julienned vegetables on the brushed paper.
5. Place the salmon on top of the vegetables, and a ¼ of the butter mixture on top of the salmon. Wrap the second part of the heart over the salmon, and fold in the ends so it forms a package that holds tight. Beat the egg in a cup using a fork, and brush the parchment paper with the egg. This will help it stick together.
6. Place the salmon packets on a sheet pan, and bake in the middle of the oven for 8–10 minutes. The packets should be golden brown and puff up in the oven.

2 cups fresh orange juice
$1/8$ vegetable bullion cube
2 tbsp chopped fresh herb, such as parsley, thyme, or marjoram
2 tbsp chopped fresh chives
3 tbsp butter
White pepper to taste

## Orange and Fresh Herb Sauce

1. Bring the orange juice and bullion to a boil in a small saucepan. Let it reduce by simmering over medium heat without a lid for 20 minutes.
2. When reduced, add the fresh herbs, chives, and pepper to taste.
3. Remove the pot from the heat and add the butter. Stir until the butter has melted and the sauce has a glossy finish.

*Serving tip!*
Serve the individual packet to each guest. It's very dramatic when each guest gets to open their own packet and this will also keep the fish warm until serving time. This recipe also tastes great with the savory waffles and horseradish cream.

*Simplify:*
You can save time by making one large salmon packet, or even buying smoked salmon that you serve with the orange sauce.

*For a challenge:*
If you're feeling really ambitious, pan-smoke your own salmon using wood chips.

# SPINACH AND ASPARAGUS SALAD WITH POACHED EGGS

**Serves 4 guests**

¾ lb fresh baby spinach
10 red pearl onions—can
    be substituted with 1
    chopped red onion
1 bunch of asparagus
1 tbsp unsalted butter
4 tbsp olive oil
4 tbsp lemon juice
Salt and pepper to taste

1. Wash and clean the baby spinach. Dry it completely in a salad spinner or using paper towels. Place in your salad bowl.
2. Peel and cut the onions and add to the spinach.
3. Clean and break off the lower part of the asparagus. Cut it into smaller pieces.
4. Add the butter to a frying pan. Once hot, add the asparagus and sauté for about four minutes.
5. Take the pan off the heat, and add the olive oil and lemon juices. Season with salt and pepper to taste, then add the asparagus. Pour pan's contents on top of the salad.

*Tip!*
The bottom part of the asparagus stem is hard and should be removed before serving. To know exactly where to cut it off, break each asparagus by holding each end and letting it snap on its own. It will naturally break off at the right part—pretty cool, huh?

2 tsp salt
2 tsp vinegar
4 eggs

## Poached Eggs

1. Fill a large pot halfway with water and bring it to a boil. Add the salt and vinegar, and reduce the heat to a simmer.
2. Carefully break one egg into a cup. Make sure that the yolk does not break. Slowly and carefully add the egg to the simmering water, and then repeat the procedure with the rest of the eggs.
3. Let the eggs simmer for 3–5 minutes, depending on how runny you like them. Serve them directly over the salad or put them in an ice bath for later serving.

*Serving tip!*
Serve the eggs in individual ramekins. It looks very festive and the eggs keep warm longer.

*Simplify:*
To save on time, clean and cut the asparagus and spinach the day before. Keep it in a bowl filled with water until you are ready to make the salad so it stays crisp and fresh.

*For a challenge:*
Try adding other vegetables to the salad. Just like the waffles, this works great with salmon.

# YOGURT RICE PUDDING WITH GRILLED FRUIT SKEWERS

**Serves 4 guests**

2 portions of risotto rice, such
    as Arborio rice
½ cup whipping cream
½ cup of plain yogurt
3 tbsp sugar
1 tsp vanilla extract


Fruit of your choice
For example: pineapple,
    peach, plums, mango,
    pears, strawberries, etc.

1. Follow the instructions on the risotto rice package to make two portions of boiled rice. Exclude the salt. Let the rice cool in a bowl in the refrigerator.
2. When you are ready to serve, whip the cream and sugar until it creates stiff peaks. Add the yogurt and the vanilla extract.
3. Mix the creamy mixture with the cooled rice.


Fruit Skewers

1. Clean and cut the fruit into ½ inch cubes. Add the fruit to small wooden skewers. To enhance the flavor of the fruit, quickly grill the skewers for a minute in a grill pan or under an oven broiler.

*Serving tip!*
Serve the rice pudding in small bowls or drinking glasses. Add a skewer to each bowl and grate some nutmeg over top. A trick when serving skewers is to place half a mango, or other fruit, on the serving tray so the guests have somewhere to discard their used skewers. Not only that, but it makes it a lot easier to clean up!

*Simplify:*
Boil the rice the day before, and mix in the yogurt, vanilla, and sugar. When you are ready to serve the next day, whip the cream and fold it into the mix.

*For a challenge:*
Mix ¼ cup of raisins with 3 tbsp of spiced, dark rum. Let the raisins sit in the rum overnight. Add the this mixture to the pudding for a sweet, and slightly boozy, flavor enhancer.

# BUFFET

*Buffets can be hosted both during the day and night. This hearty menu is more suitable for an evening affair, starting between 6:00—9:00 PM.*

## MENU

Lavender and Peach Bellini

—

Salt Crusted Walnut Bread

Chèvre with Candied Figs

Wild Mushroom and Lemon Risotto

Tarragon Chicken with Anchovy Cream

Lamb Skewers with Hot Pistachio and
Mint Sauce

Tomato and Arugula Salad with Balsamic
Bacon

—

Spice Crusted Chocolate Tart with
Pineapple and Pink Peppercorn Compote

IT'S A TRIED *and true tradition to let guests serve themselves from a buffet. In the Middle Ages, banquets were the party style du jour. In 18th-century France, the modern buffet was developed and its popularity quickly spread across Europe. Then, in the early 20th century, it was strictly forbidden to serve any buffet dishes that required the use of a knife under the notion that guests should be able to eat while standing, with the plate in one hand and the fork in the other. Today, seating at a buffet is also quite common, and it is therefore acceptable to serve food that requires the use of a knife.*

## DÉCOR

Your buffet table will usually become the focus of the room, so take the time to decorate it. First off, make sure the buffet tabel is well lit, but be conservative with candles since guests can easily burn themselves when reaching to fill their plates. It's also a fire hazard, and flaming buffets are not a hit (been there, done that!). Use simple design and decorations to impress your guests. Write and frame cards explaining each dish and the ingredients included next to each course being offered. Wrap the cutlery in napkins, tying with ribbon to hold the sets together. Not only does this look nice, but it also makes it easier for the guests to carry. Place food on different levels for visual effect and easy access. Keep in mind that higher objects catch the eye first, so spend extra time on the presentations for the top level serving trays, then work your way down.

## FOOD

On average, each guest will eat approximately one pound of food from the buffet and lighter dishes, like vegetables sides, are typically more popular than heavy ones, like sides containing meat. When planning your buffet, pick dishes that will taste good even at room temperature, making sure that fifteen to twenty percent of the buffet is vegetarian to accommdoate all of your guests. Hot food can be tricky, so serve it in smaller amounts and have the serving plates changed frequently so food isn't left to get cold. If you are starting to run out of a dish, or simply don't have that much, place it toward the end of the buffet since guests tend to fill their plates towards the beginning of the buffet line. By the time they reach your least abundant dish, plates will already be full!

## SERVICE

Guests serve themselves at any buffet. For this reason, it's not always considered a very fancy way to throw an event. Guests appreciate the ability to pick their own foods, however, and as a host, it is the best way to serve a large crowd in a short amount of time. You can either serve a buffet standing or seated. A standing buffet accommodates more guests in a smaller space and requires less preparation. For a seated buffet, you can either set the tables with cutlery, napkins, and glasses—as you would for a regular dinner party—or you can place utensils on the buffet table and let your guests pick them up as they get food. Set up the buffet table close to the kitchen to avoid the crowd when replenishing the serving plates. When a serving plate is half-empty, exchange it for a new one—the exception here being unless there is a rush. In that case, you can let the plates empty completely before you bring out a new one. If your buffet party is a larger event, plan on having two extra plates with food prepped in the kitchen for each dish: one plate filled with food ready for serving, and the other half-full. Swap the serving plate on the buffet for the full plate when it is half finished.

In the kitchen, transfer the leftovers from the buffet serving plate to the new, half-full plate. Serving utensils should be placed on small plates lined with a napkin in front of each dish. If you want to be fancy, use tongs for the bread. One modern buffet trend is to use TV-dinner plates with separate compartments for each dish—believe it or not, it's so ugly that it looks cool!

## BUFFET TYPES

### One-Sided Buffet

Set up your buffet table against a wall so that the food is served only from one side. This works great for a normal-sized buffet, hosted in your home. When space is tight, use a round table placed in the middle of the room for your buffet.

### Double-Sided Buffet

When hosting a bigger party, serve a double-sided buffet to avoid long lines. Place the table, and utensils, so that the guests can approach from both sides.

### Stations

Split up the buffet by setting up food stations throughout the space. One station for courses served at room temperature, one for food served warm, and a separate for serving desserts. This option helps you accommodate large groups, creates a good flow in the space, or spreads out your guests in bigger venues.

## DRINKS

Before the guests indulge in your buffet, it's nice to welcome them with a tasty cocktail or two. The buffet in the book highlights the Italian flavors, so the Bellini is a perfect starter. Created in 1948 by Giuseppe Cipriani, the original recipe for the Bellini was made with white peach purée, a rare fruit that ripens for only four months every year. Serve each guest and apertif cocktail, like the Bellini, then let them dig in!

For the buffet, feel free to place wine and beverages directly on the dinner table. Another option is to set up a separate beverage station for wine, water, nonalcoholic alternatives, and glasses.

### How Much Will Your Guest Eat?

| | |
|---|---|
| Meat, bird, or fish | 6 oz. |
| Potato, rice, pasta, bread | 5 oz. |
| Vegetables | 5 oz. |
| Total | 16 oz. |

### In the Right Order

To ensure that the buffet runs smoothly, organize it as follows:

1. Plates
2. Salads and dressings
3. Smaller courses and their sides
4. Main courses and their sides
5. Bread
6. Butter, salt and pepper
7. Cutlery and glasses

# *LAVENDER AND PEACH BELLINI*

1 part peach purée
2 parts Prosecco or another
sparkling wine
1 pinch of edible, dried or
fresh lavender

1. Place the purée in the bottom of a Champagne glass or flute.
2. Carefully pour in the sparkling wine.
3. Don't stir, but rather use a spoon to pull the purée up along the sides of the glass, so that you wont lose the bubbles.
4. Decorate with the lavender.

*Tip!*
If you are having a hard time finding peach purée, you can also use high-quality peach juice or other fruit puree. A classic Bellini is topped off with peach liquor.

  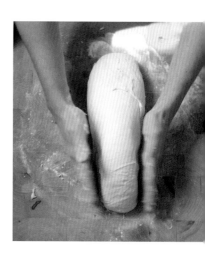

# SALT CRUSTED WALNUT BREAD

¼ oz. bag of yeast
2 cups lukewarm water
2 tsp salt
2 tbsp honey
½ cup olive oil
½ cup peeled walnuts
5 cups flour
Sea salt

1. In a large mixing bowl or stand mixer, add the yeast, lukewarm water, salt, honey, and ¾ of the olive oil. Stir and let the yeast dissolve and activate.
2. Roughly chop the walnuts, and mix in the batter together with the flour. Add a little at a time, while mixing in a processor for 5 minutes, or by hand for 10 minutes. It should have a loose consistency when done.
3. Let the dough rise, under a tea towel in a warm draft-free place until it has doubled in size.
4. Puncture the dough with a fork so the air can escape. Let it rise to double the size a second time, and puncture again. Wash and flour your hands, and place the dough onto a sheet pan lined with parchment paper. Shape it into a ball, adding flour as necessary to keep from sticking.
5. Preheat your oven to 475°F.
6. Let the dough rise a third time to double the size on the sheet pan covered with a tea towel.
7. Brush the dough with the remaining olive oil and add a few teaspoons of sea salt to the top.
8. Bake the bread in the middle rack of the oven for approximately 15 minutes. Lower the temp to 300°F and let it bake for an additional 40 minutes.

*Serving tip!*
You can skip the butter with this bread, since it has an olive oil and salted crust. It works well served with cheese on the buffet.

*Simplify:*
Home baked bread is a great addition to any meal, but if you're short on time opt for ready-made nut bread at the bakery, and dampen the crust. Heat in the oven for 5 minutes for a fresh-baked taste.

*For a challenge:*
Individual portions are always a crowd pleaser. Make rolls from the same recipe, and while you're at it, freeze a few for other occasions. Save for up to three months in the freezer.

# CHÈVRE WITH CANDIED FIGS

**Serves 4 guests**

¾ pound chèvre or other
   goat cheese
4 fresh figs or ½ cup dried
¼ cup of balsamic vinegar
3 tbsp of brown muscovado
   or brown sugar
Prosciutto or un-cured

1. Slice the chèvre log, and place on a sheet pan. Cut the figs into rounds.
2. Pour the balsamic vinegar and sugar into a small saucepan, and bring it to a boil. Lower the heat and let it simmer until the mixture is reduced and sticks to the back of a spoon.
3. If you are using dried figs, place them in the vinegar mixture and let them absorb some of the fluid while the mixture cools.
4. Heat the chèvre cheese slices quickly by using your oven's broiler function for about 3 minutes, or until the cheese has slightly started to melt. Place the cheese on a serving plate, and top it with the candied figs and vinegar mixture. Serve warm with ham and fresh, crispy bread.

*Simplify:*
You can replace muscavado sugar with brown sugar, honey, or granulated white sugar. Always taste first, since the different sugars have different sweetnesses, and you might need to adjust the quantity.

*For a challenge:*
With their peppery honey flavor, Black Mission are the best figs money can buy. Fresh Black Mission figs are only available a few weeks out of the year, so if you happen to come across some, make a couple batches of compote and freeze for use throughout the year.

*Muscovado sugar*
Muscovado sugar is raw sugar made from sugar canes. It comes in both light and dark varieties and, compared with refined sugar, has a higher mineral content. The darker sugar has a flavor similar to licorice, while the lighter version has a flavor similar to toffee.

# WILD MUSHROOM AND LEMON RISOTTO

**Serves 4 guests**

½ cup of dried mixed wild
    mushrooms
4 cups of chicken or
    vegetable stock
2 large shallots
2 tbsp olive oil
1 cup of risotto rice, such
    as Arborio rice
⅓ cup white wine
¼ cup heavy cream
¼ cup grated parmesan
    cheese
2 tbsp lemon zest
Salt and pepper to taste

1. Place the dried mushrooms in a small saucepan, and add enough water to just cover the mushrooms. Bring it to a boil, then remove from the heat and let it steep for one hour. Strain the mushrooms, reserving the mushrooms and add it to the stock for flavor.
2. Heat the stock. Peel and finely chop the shallots. Roughly chop the mushrooms.
3. In a large heavy-bottom pan, heat the olive oil. Add the shallots, mushrooms, and rice and sauté over medium heat until the rice is translucent.
4. Add the wine to the mixture. Stir with a wooden spoon until most of the fluid has been absorbed.
5. Add the stock, ¼ cup at a time. Bring to boil over medium heat and stir constantly until most of the stock has been absorbed. Repeat until all the stock has been added; this should take about 20 minutes.
6. When the rice is al dente it's ready to be served. Add the cream, Parmesan cheese, mushrooms, and lemon zest. Salt and pepper to taste.

*Serving tip!*
Serve the risotto either straight out of the pan or in large hollowed-out cheese wheel. Serving out of cheese is a fun alternative and also adds flavor to the risotto when it melts. Choose a hard flavorful cheese such as manchego or parmesan.

*Simplify:*
Risotto is a simple dish, great for serving at a buffet. Best of all, it can be varied a million different ways—just make sure it's prepared close to serving time. Even though simple to make, risotto does demand a lot of attention and needs to be stirred constantly Recruit a friend to stir while you prepare the rest of the buffet. In case of an emergency, you can always prepare in advance and place under foil in the oven. Just add a little more cream right before serving.

*For a challenge:*
The stock, not the wine, is what makes the risotto. If you want to show off, make your own stock. Use leftover chicken with bones, celery, onion, carrots, parsley, peppercorns, and bay leaves. Let simmer for at least an hour, strain, and you've got delicious, homemade chicken stock.

*Risotto Rice!*
Since risotto rice absorbs fluid better than regular rice, it can be stirred longer and releases more starch, which gives the risotto its nice creamy texture. The most famous and popular risotto rices are from Italy, like Arborio or Carnaroli.

# TARRAGON CHICKEN WITH ANCHOVY CREAM

**Serves 4 guests**

12 oz, about 2 boneless
chicken breasts
(approx. 2)
2 tbsp chopped tarragon
2 tbsp lemon juice
1 tbsp olive oil
Salt and pepper to taste
4 chopsticks, for serving

1 tbsp olive oil
2 anchovy fillets in oil
1 tsp lemon zest
2 tbsp lemon juice
½ cup crème fraiche
2 tbsp grated Parmesan
cheese
1 pinch tarragon
Salt and pepper to taste

1. Cut the chicken breast into 1-inch cubes. Place in a zip-top bag with the remaining ingredients. Seal and let marinate in the refrigerator for at least an hour.
2. Turn your oven to broil and skewer the cubes on the chopsticks. If using nonlacquered chopsticks, then place them in water for an hour before use, so they won't char in the oven.
3. Grill the skewers under the broiler for about 12 minutes, or until completely cooked through. Turn after half the time.

### Anchovy Cream

1. Heat the olive oil in a small saucepan. Add the anchovy fillets and stir them until they melt.
2. Remove the saucepan from the heat and add the rest of the ingredients. Salt and pepper to taste. Add more lemon juice if you want.

### Serving tip!
The skewers can be served both warm and cold.

### Simplify:
The sauce tastes better the longer it gets to absorb the flavors, so it can easily be prepared the day before. The same goes for the marinated skewers. Prepare and marinate the day before, grilling just before the guests arrive.

### For a challenge:
If you have access to a grill, then of course that adds to the flavor. Don't forget to soak nonlacquered skewers beforehand so that they don't catch fire.

# LAMB SKEWERS WITH HOT MINT AND PISTACHIO SAUCE

**Serves 4 guests**

12 oz of tender, boneless
lamb shoulder
2 garlic cloves
3 tbsp lemon juice
Salt and pepper to taste
4 chopsticks, lacquered for
color

½ cup mint gel
¼ cup pistachio nuts
Cayenne, white and black
Salt and pepper to taste

*1. Same preparation as chicken skewers*

### Hot Mint and Pistachio Sauce

1. Peel and chop the pistachios. Add to a small saucepan and roast for 2 minutes or until hot. Lower the heat and add the mint jelly, letting it melt over low heat.
2. Add the peppers to taste. By stirring the peppers, they will cook more evenly.

### Serving tip!
You can serve the skewers standing up by skewering them in half a fruit, such as a grapefruit.

### Fact!
Grain-fed lamb has a much less gamey flavor than the grass-fed lamb. So if you usually don't like lamb because it is gamey, try grain-fed instead!

# *TOMATO AND ARUGULA SALAD WITH BALSAMIC BACON*

**Serves 4 guests**

5 thick slices of bacon
¼ cup of balsamic vinegar
4 tbsp of muscovado sugar
½ pound of cherry tomatoes
½ mango, cubed
1 small red onion
¾ pound of arugula
Salt and pepper to taste
Edible flowers for decorating
    (optional)

1. Cut the bacon slices into 1-inch pieces, and fry until crispy. To make it crispier and get rid of excess grease, let it sit on a paper towel when done.
2. When the bacon is done, turn off the heat. Carefully add the sugar and then the vinegar to the pan. Watch out for splashes. Salt and pepper to taste.
3. Cut the tomatoes into halves, peel and cut the mango into small cubes, and finely chop the red onion. Add the arugula to your serving bowl. Then add the vinaigrette from the pan and toss well. Finally add the other vegetables and bacon bits.

*Simplify:*
Prepare the vinaigrette and bacon the day before, and simply heat before serving.

*For a challenge:*
This dressing works great with a lot of different salad combinations, as long as the base of the salad is arugula or spinach, which can take the heat. For a beautiful touch, try decorating with some colorful edible flowers from your local grocery store.

*Tip!*
In this recipe, bacon fat is used instead of oil in the vinaigrette. As a healthy alternative, drain some of the fat from the pan before mixing the vinaigrette in the pan.

# SPICE CRUSTED CHOCOLATE TART WITH PINEAPPLE AND PINK PEPPERCORN COMPOTE

**Serves 4 guests**

4 tbsp unsalted butter
2½ cups of crushed
    graham cracker or
    digestive crackers
    (crumbs)
1½ cups of crushed ginger
    snaps
2 tbsp cacao powder
½ cup sugar


12 oz. dark chocolate,
    preferably 60 %
    cacao content like
    Valhona
7 oz. butter
5 egg whites
5 egg yolks
¼ sugar
1¼ heavy cream
3 tbsp cognac (optional)

1. Preheat your oven to 425°F. Meanwhile, melt the butter. Crush the crackers and ginger snaps. Mix all the ingredients in a bowl. Add some extra melted butter if the dough gets dry.
2. Using your fingers, press the dough out into a round cake pan 8–10 inches wide. Bake the crust in the middle of the oven for about 15 minutes. When done let the crust cool, and then transfer it to the freezer.


### Chocolate Filling

1. Melt the chocolate and butter in the microwave, stirring every 30 seconds until it is a smooth mixture.
2. Let the mixture cool slightly, and then add the egg yokes one at a time while stirring.
3. Beat the egg whites until they create stiff peaks. Add the sugar and beat until hard and white.
4. Carefully stir in the egg-white mixture to the chocolate mixture. Let it cool in the refrigerator.
5. Whip the cream until stiff, and then add to the chocolate mixture. Add the cognac and return to the refrigerator.
6. Remove the crust from the freezer and add the chocolate filling to the crust. Keep the tart in the fridge until serving.


*Serving tip!*
It can be messy cutting a mousse tart. Put the knife under hot running water for a smooth and easy cut.


1 cup pineapple juice
3 tbsp pink peppercorns
4 tbsp sugar
10 oz. of fresh pineapple

### Pineapple and Pink Peppercorn Compote

1. Combine the pineapple juice, sugar, and peppercorns in a small saucepan. Simmer over medium heat for about 20 minutes until the liquid has reduced.
2. Remove the saucepan from the heat. Chop the pineapple into small cubes and add to the sauce.


*Simplify:*
Instead of baking the pie crust, you can simply freeze it and add the filling right before serving.


*For a challenge:*
Individual servings are always great for parties, so use the same recipe but bake in smaller ramekins. Experiment with different flavored compotes. Try peach and liquorice, strawberry and mint, or raspberry and balsamic vinegar.

# DINNER

*Starts between 6:00 PM and 9:00 PM*
*A seated dinner can be as elegant or as cozy as you like. Choose from menu ideas below.*

## MENU

### Appetizers
Champagne & Oyster Bouillabaisse
Roasted Acorn Squash & Onion Soup Au Gratin

### Entrees
Roast Veal Chop on the bone with
Preserved-Lemon Gremolata
Calvados Roast Chicken with Lady Apples
& Garlic Bulbs

### Side Dishes
Pommes Anna
Roasted Carrots with Fennel Seed
& Curry Oil

### Dessert
Port Wine and Red Peppercorn Ice Cream
with Rhubarb Compote

*WHAT WE TODAY consider festive food originated as Grande Cuisine in 18th-century France. Hosts loved to show off their prestige and class, and Grande Cuisine was the ultimate symbol of wealth. It was a sport to make cooking as long and complicated as possible, and a single dinner could consist of over a dozen dishes, expensive ingredients, and loads of exotic spices. Since spices were imported from abroad, they were extremely expensive. The more used in a dish, the more luxurious it was considered to be, with no thought to the flavor or taste.*

*After the French revolution in 1789 and subsequent fall of the aristocrats, dishes were simplified and became accessible to everyone. The new cuisine was dubbed Cuisine Classique and was spearheaded by Auguste Escoffier, the father of modern cooking. Today's style of cooking is called Nouvelle Cuisine, and shies away from overpowering food with lots of spices and sauces. Instead, it focuses on enhancing ingredients' natural flavors.*

## DÉCOR

When hosting a dinner, focus on designing a great table. After all, you and your guests will be spending a few hours there, and it is often all the décor you need. A nicely set table looks inviting and enhances the dinner experience by stimulating all the senses. In the chapter "Table Setting" (p. 50-63), you'll find tips, ideas, and guidelines for how to set your dinner table. Use it as an inspiration when planning your table design.

## FOOD

The first step in creating a great menu is to utilize ingredients that are in season. Not only do they have the best flavor, but it also keeps your budget down. Put your old food magazines and cookbooks to use when searching for ideas for your menu.

Let the recipes inspire you, and be creative. Pick your favorite sauce from one magazine and the stuffed chicken breast from another. Always simplify the preparation as much as possible when composing party menus to avoid stress. When you've decided on your menu, write it down and make sure your courses work well together. The key is to vary different flavors, but still manage to match them as a whole. Colors should also be taken into consideration; colorful dishes stimulate the senses. Make sure your courses have diverse textures. For example, if you are serving a pork tenderloin with a cream sauce, maybe you should reconsider serving a creamy soup as well. Why not go for a tomato-based soup instead? Don't forget to incorporate your party's theme. When it's time to hit the grocery store, divide your shopping list into different columns for meat, fish, dairy, produce, and dry goods. This will save you time, and keep you from running back and forth from section to section. Bring a calculator so you can easily calculate quantities, and double-check how many containers you might need of a certain ingredient. Prepare as much of the food as possible the day before the party.

# SERVICE

If you aim to be a perfect hostess there are a few guidelines to stick to when you are serving your guests. Most etiquette rules are common sense and originated for practical reasons.

*- Guest of Honor*
The lady seated to the right of the host is the guest of honor and should be served each course first. Continue service counterclockwise, ending with the host.

*- Enjoy!*
When hot food is served at a table with more than eight people, the guests are welcome to dig in as soon they've been served. If not, they should wait until everyone at the table has been served their food.

*- To the left*
Plated food is served from the left of the guest, starting with the guest of honor and ending with the host.

*- To the right*
Beverages are served from the right, and dirty dishes are removed this way as well.

# DRINKS

Dinner is commonly accompanied by wine. When serving wine you should also serve water, without ice, since it freezes the taste buds and makes them less sensitive to flavors. Pair the appetizer in this chapter with a robust white or light red wine, and serve a spicy red wine with the flavorful main course. For dessert, a sweet white wine (like ice wine) is recommended. A brave hostess can experiment by pairing teas with her dinner instead.

## A Short Wine Guide

*Temperature.*
In general, we serve our white wines too cold, and our reds too warm. 45°F to 55°F is the right temperature range to serve a white wine, as well as champagne and sparkling wine. If you happen to have a lower quality white wine, serve it colder to mask its taste. Red wines are preferably served at 50°F and 60°F. Red wine has heavier molecules than white and therefore requires a higher temperature for the bouquet to blossom. The theory of room temperature reds is incorrect since it actually refers to temperatures in wine cellars.

*Wine and food pairing?*
Traditionally white wine is served with lighter and milder foods like vegetarian dishes, fish, chicken, seafood, and turkey. Red wine accompanies dishes with heavier and stronger flavors such as grilled fatty fish, goose, duck, pork, lamb, and beef. However, taste is subjective and these are just guidelines. Today, people experiment more often with wine, and so should you. Give the chardonnay a rest, and try a light red with that fish dish instead.

*Quantity?*
Etiquette dictates you fill a wine glass no more than three quarters of the way. You may want to serve even less white wine so it stays cool as your guest finishes the glass.

## Keep a Party Diary

A hostess on top of her game keeps a party-book where she logs guest lists, menus, recipes, decorations, themes etc. This way she will avoid party faux pas, such as serving her favorite seafood skewer three times in a row to the same guest.

## Seasonal Foods

*Spring:*
asparagus, artichokes, apricots, avocado, carrots, mango, new potatoes, strawberry, spinach

*Summer:*
beets, blackberries, blueberries, broccoli, corn, cucumbers, nectarines, tomatoes, peaches, plums, zucchini

*Fall:*
cauliflower, apples, figs, garlic, ginger, grapes, mushrooms, parsnips, sweet potatoes, pomegranate, pears, pumpkins

*Winter:*
grapefruit, kale, lemons, oranges, radishes, turnips

## Food Allergies

Ask guests to RSVP with possible food allergies and vegetarian preferences.

## Three Courses for the Stressed-Out Host

Home-cooked meals are always greatly appreciated, especially in today's take-out society. If you really detest cooking or are short on time, but don't want to skimp on that homemade feel, a great compromise is to make an easy appetizer and dessert, and order out for the main course. Hide the take-out carton, and no one will be the wiser.

# CHAMPAGNE & OYSTER BOULLABAISE

**Serves 4 guests**

12 oysters
2 tbsp butter
5 shallots, finely
  chopped
1 yellow onion,
  finely chopped
1 celery stalk, finely
  chopped
¼ cup cognac
3 cups fish stock
¼ vegetable bullion
  cube
1 bay leaf
White pepper
¼ tsp cayenne pepper
2 cups Champagne or
  dry, sparkling wine
1 cup  heavy cream
¼ cup chives, finely
  chopped
Sea salt to taste

1. Scrub the oysters under water well, and check that they close when handled—this means they are fresh and alive.
2. Melt the butter in a large pot and the onions and celery until translucent. Add the cognac and let it boil.
3. Add the stock, bullion cube, bay leaf, white and cayenne peppers. Simmer for 40 minutes on low heat.
4. Add the ¾ of the Champagne and the cream. Let it boil for 10 minutes. U p to now you can prep this in advance.
5. Reheat the pot 10 minutes before serving. Add chives and remaining Champagne. Season with salt and pepper, if needed.
6. Add the oysters and let boil just until the oysters have opened and put in the middle of the table so guests can serve themselves.

# ROASTED ACORN SQUASH & ONION SOUP AU GRATIN

**Serves 4 guests**

4 small acorn squash
2 cups fresh mushrooms, such as chanterelles
1 yellow onion, chopped
½ stick unsalted butter
3 cups store-bought French onion soup
1 cup grated cheese, such as Gruyere
1 cup French bread, cubed
Salt and pepper to taste

1. Sauté mushrooms in a frying pan in 2 tbsp butter. Add salt and pepper to taste, then reserve and toast bread cubes.
2. Heat store-bought French onion soup with mushrooms. Set aside.
3. Wash acorn squash, cut off and save the tops. Remove squash seeds with spoon and place "lid" back on each squash. If they don't stand up straight, then cut bottom slightly with a bread knife so they stand upright. Melt remaining butter. Brush inside and outside of squash with butter. Place on a baking sheet.
4. Fill with soup mixture then bake in oven for 30 minutes at 350°F or until squash flesh is tender. Add bread crumbs, and cheese on top. Bake for an additional 10 minutes at 400°F, or until golden and crispy. Serve hot.

# ROAST VEAL CHOP ON THE BONE WITH PRESERVED LEMON GREMOLATA

**Serves 4 guests**

5 veal chops
3 tbsp unsalted butter, melted
Sea salt and pepper to taste

Peel of 1 preserved lemon
1 bunch parsley
1 tbsp fleur de sel (sea salt)
3 tbsp unsalted butter, melted

1. Preheat your oven to 400°F. Brush the steak with melted butter and salt & pepper well.
2. Put the veal chop in the oven for about 15 minutes to get a good color. Lower the heat to 300°F and let it roast for about 45 minutes, or until a meat thermometer reads 160°F.
3. Take out of the oven and wrap it in foil and let it rest for 15 minutes before serving.

### Preserved-Lemon Gremolata

1. Combine the lemon and parsley to a food processor and give it a chop.
2. Mix in the butter by hand.
3. Add the gremolata on top of each steak. Serve the rest on the table with the roast.

### Tip!
If you don't have preserved lemon, then use the skin of organic lemons. Just make sure to wash well before using for this recipe.

# CALVADOS ROAST CHICKEN WITH LADY APPLES & GARLIC BULBS

**Serves 4 guests**

1 chicken, washed
    and dried
2 bulbs garlic
3 small apples,
    such as Red Lady
    or Gala
2 tbsp rose
    peppercorns
3 tbsp calvados,
    or other brandy
½ stick unsalted butter
3 tbsp dark soy sauce,
    such as mushroom-
    flavored soy sauce
1 lemon
5 prunes
5 sprigs fresh thyme
1 cup heavy cream
Sea salt and pepper
    to taste

1. Preheat the oven to 375°F.
2. Cut the garlic bulbs and apples in half, then place in the bottom of a large oven-safe dish.
3. Cut the lemon in half, rub the chicken with lemon halves, squeezing gently to coat bird in juice.
4. Salt the inside of the bird, then fill with lemon halves, prunes, fresh thyme, and calvados.
5. Place chicken in the dish, arranging the garlic and apples around the bird.
6. Melt the butter and mix with rose pepper and soy. Brush the chicken with the mixture. Salt and pepper on top.
7. Place chicken in oven and let crisp for 10 minutes. Brush with more of the soy/butter mixture. Reduce oven temperature to 350°F and let roast for about 35 minutes, depending on chicken size. Continue basting bird every 10-15 minutes, checking for doneness by inserting a knife by the thigh and see if juices run clear.
8. Let rest for 5 minutes before serving. In a small saucepan, mix the amazing pan drippings with cream and salt and pepper. Serve remaining glaze as a sauce.

# POMMES ANNA

**Serves 4 guests**

6 medium potatoes
1 stick unsalted butter,
melted

1. Preheat your oven to 325°F and butter a round cake dish.
2. Peel the potatoes and slice them and thin as possible. Try using a food processor.
3. Dry the potato slices.
4. Start on the edges, and place the slices in a circle to create a first layer, then brush with melted butter. Season with salt & pepper.
5. Repeat the process about 5 times, or until dish is full.
6. Bake in the oven for about an hour, or until tender and golden brown on top.
7. Remove from oven and allow to cool slightly before serving. To serve, flip upside down and serve in slices like a cake.

# *ROASTED CARROTS WITH FENNEL SEED & CURRY OIL*

**Serves 4 guests**

2 bunches carrots,
  cleaned
3 tbsp olive oil
2 tsp curry powder
1 tbsp fennel seed
Sea salt and pepper
  to taste

1. Preheat your oven to 350°F.
2. Combine curry powder, oil and fennel seed in a bowl.
3. Toss carrots in oil on a sheet pan and then bake for about 20 minutes, or until roasted.

# PORT WINE & RED PEPPERCORN ICE CREAM WITH RHUBARB COMPOTE

3 cups of vanilla ice cream
1 cup of port wine
3 tbsp red peppercorns
¾ cup of sugar

6 stalks rhubarb
1 ½ fresh strawberries
1 ½ cups sugar

1. Heat sugar and port wine in a small saucepan with the peppercorns for about 10 minutes until thick. Set aside to cool.

**Rhubarb-Strawberry Compote**

1. Clean stalks by peeling off outer layers. Chop in ½-inch pieces. Clean and cut the strawberries into quarters.
2. Heat with sugar and a ½ cup of water in the saucepan. Simmer for about 20 minutes until soft and a thicker soup-like consistency.
3. Serve rhubarb compote with a scoop of ice cream and the port wine syrup.

Acknowledgments

Thank you to my family, friends, and colleagues for all your support, taste-testing, and modeling throughout this entire project. To Ingela Holm & Bill Wolfstahl: thank you for picking up the project and making it into a successful book. Thank you to my mother who is my all-around kitchen inspiration, Margareta who always knew I would write a cookbook and Robert Andersson & Jared Levan—my amazing editors who tirelessly helped me create a great text, despite my dyslexia.

Special thanks to:

– Daniel Walsh for all his help & support
– Whole Foods for having the best grocery store in town
– Union Square Greenmarket and all their vendors
– Mateus, Royal Copenhagen, Le Creuset, ABC Carpet, Bodum, and Anthropologie for equipment and props
– Sun West Studios & Jennifer Ohlsson who not only is a great friend but has a wonderful apartment she always lets me borrow
– LP Fashion Philosophy
– Ronnie Peterson at Next for his amazing hair and make-up skills
– Everyone at the New York Flower Market for putting up with us taking pictures, especially Ruth Fischl, Fischer Page & G Page
– Thank you Morgan Norman. You are the sweetest rocker I know, and a great photographer. Thanks for taking a wonderful picture.

Most of all, thank you for taking the time to read this book. I hope it inspires you to plan some memorable dinners, parties, and other events. For even more ideas, check out what I am cooking on my website: www. linnea-johansson.com